THE GREATEST
STORY EVER SOLD

THE GREATEST STORY EVER SOLD

*A Considered and Whimsical Illumination
of the Really Good Parts of Holy Writ*

Reed Martin and Austin Tichenor

With a Foreword by
Austin Tichenor

And a Backword by
Reed Martin

Westminster John Knox Press
Louisville, Kentucky

Book design by Sharon Adams
Cover design by Kathy York
Cover illustration by Dennis L. McKinsey

First edition

Published by Westminster John Knox Press
Louisville, Kentucky

This book is printed on acid-free paper that meets the American National Standards Institute Z39.48 standard. ∞

PRINTED IN THE UNITED STATES OF AMERICA

01 02 03 04 05 06 07 08 09 10 — 10 9 8 7 6 5 4 3 2 1

Library of Congress Cataloging-in-Publication Data

Martin, Reed.
   The greatest story ever sold : a considered and whimsical illumination of the really good parts of holy writ / Reed Martin and Austin Tichenor ; with a foreword by Austin Tichenor and a backword by Reed Martin.
      p. cm.
   Includes bibliographical references.
   ISBN 0-664-25805-0 (alk. paper)
   1. Bible—Introductions. 2. Bible—Humor. I. Tichenor, Austin. II. Title.

BS475.3 .M37 2001
220'.02'07—dc21

00-050461

About the Authors

Reed Martin has coauthored three plays with the Reduced Shakespeare Company—*The Complete History of America (abridged)*, *The Bible: The Complete Word of God (abridged)*, and *The Complete Millennium Musical (abridged)* and contributed additional material to *The Complete Works of William Shakespeare (abridged)*. He has written for the BBC, National Public Radio, Britain's Channel Four, RTE Ireland, Public Radio International, the *Washington Post*, and *Vogue*. Prior to joining the Reduced Shakespeare Company, Reed was a clown and assistant ringmaster with Ringling Brothers/Barnum & Bailey Circus. He has a B.A. in political science and theater from UC Berkeley and an M.F.A. in acting from UC San Diego. He lives in Northern California with his wife and sons.

Austin Tichenor cowrote and costarred in the stage comedies *The Complete History of America (abridged)*, *The Bible: The Complete Word of God (abridged)*, and *The Complete Millennium Musical (abridged)*; the half-hour TV film *The Ring Reduced*; and the radio productions of *The Reduced Shakespeare Radio Show* (BBC), *The Reduced Shakespeare Company Round Table* (NPR's *All Things Considered*), and *The Reduced Shakespeare Company Christmas* (Public Radio International). He is also the author of over twenty plays and musicals for young audiences, and once had a letter to the editor published in the *New York Times Book Review*. He's not proud of it, but he was young and needed the money. He lives in Los Angeles where he is hard at work on three screenplays, a novel, and his wife.

To Oprah Winfrey,
whose Book Club continues to awaken America
(and indeed, the world) to the beauty of language
and the power of the written word.
You go, girlfriend!

And also to the Reverend Alan Knudsen,
whose guidance and inspiration made this book possible.
Get well soon.

Table of Contents

Acknowledgments

I gratefully acknowledge the input of two scholars who gave freely of their time and expertise: Richard Fulcher, professor of Victorian musicology at the California College of Applied Mechanics, who shared with me his knowledge of and passion for the rhododendron in all its complexity; and Dee Ryan, who liked it.

Austin Tichenor
July 2000

I would like to thank Dr. Davis Perkins of Westminster John Knox Press for his extraordinary patience and guidance. I still can't quite believe he agreed to publish this book. There really is no accounting for taste.

And special thanks to my loving wife, Jane Martin, without whom my marriage would be extremely lonely.

Reed Martin
July 2000

Foreword

Chaos

AUSTIN

In the beginning was the Word. And the Word was . . . *bandwagon*.

As in the expression, "hop on the bandwagon."

The Bible is the most popular book in the world, for many reasons. It's an inspiration to millions of people around the world, the cornerstone of many of your most popular religions, and the Word of God transcribed by Man, for Man.

Most importantly, though, it's a great story, wonderfully told. And loaded with sex and violence.

It should therefore come as no surprise to discover that the Bible is the greatest non–Harry Potter related phenomenon in the history of publishing. Not only has it never been out of print since it was first published and became widely available in the sixteenth century, but more books have been written *about* the Bible than any other book in history. The Bible is the greatest book in the history of literature. Similarly, the book you are currently holding in your hands is the greatest book you are currently holding in your hands.

The Bible and its related books of criticism and observation have generated millions—probably even billions—of dollars for devout authors like us. Contrary to what you may discover, we are not fools. We want to *leap* on this bandwagon.

Because the funny thing is, not many people have actually read the entire Bible. Let's face it—it's a tough read. The language is either archaic or, depending on your New Revised Contemporary Translation, disturbingly updated. ("And Moses said to Pharaoh, 'Let my people, you know, do their own thing.'") It's filled with odd-sounding names, unbelievable miracles, and some really terrible weather. Plus—let's be honest—it gets a little preachy.

All of which is a shame, because the Bible is also filled with rip-roaring adventure, ferocious battles, more sex than *Playboy*, more violence than Tom Clancy, more bigamy than Utah, and more ghosts and angels and mentions of Maine than Stephen King.

This is where we come in. We want to tell you about all the good stuff in the Bible. Not the stuff that's good *for* you—we mean the stuff you may have missed while reading the parts you *had* to read. The *real* reasons the Bible is the greatest story ever sold. We want to show you the hidden treasures of the Bible.

And when we say *we*, we don't mean the omniscient editorial royal *we*. We mean we, the two of us, Reed Martin and Austin Tichenor. We are authors and scholars who have been friends and collaborators for more than twenty years. Between the two of us, we have read almost the entire Bible. In the original English.

Austin is a pagan. Okay, that's putting it too harshly. He's a jerk. (That's pretty harsh too, but while not inaccurate is beside the point.) At various times, Austin has been an Atheist (lapsed), a Pantheist (reformed), and is now a practicing Utilitarian. He believes in God when it's useful.

Reed is a Presbyterian. This is a little like saying he's a chair: it sounds revealing but it's not actually enlightening. (He is, however, surprisingly comfortable to sit on.) He's a man wracked by guilt, which is odd because he's not Jewish and he hasn't done anything. Seriously, the man hasn't done *anything*. Go ahead, ask his mother. She'll tell you straight to your face, "Reed who?"

We both married Irish-Catholics, if that helps. If nothing else, it shows a willingness to obey and tolerate extremist points of view.

We say all this in the interest of full disclosure. You don't want to buy this book only to get home and say, "Oh, my (nondenominationally specific) God! What the H-E-double-hockey-sticks have I done?" It's important to know what you're getting into.

This book is very much a team effort. We consulted with each other several times a day, mostly regarding fashion tips, but frequently about the progress of the book. For further clarity, we divided the actual writing of the book in half. Reed wrote the odd chapters. I wrote the odder chapters.

This book is in many ways a quest. A quest for the hidden treasures of the Bible; a quest for the meaning of the Greatest Story Ever Sold; a quest for an unmixed metaphor; a quest for personal discovery and social relevance; and finally, a quest for spiritual salvation, if you will.

And even if you won't.

Please turn the page. Let's get questing.

Chapter One

Creation

The Six-Day Work Week, and What's the Deal with the Platypus?

REED

G enesis. The Beginning. A very good place to start. Genesis is the first of the five books of the Pentateuch—the first five books of the Bible. *Pentateuch* translates as "the law" or "to teach." Maybe it's just me, but "the law" and "to teach" seem like significantly different translations of the word *Pentateuch*. This clearly indicates that the scholars doing the translating didn't really know what the dickens *Pentateuch* means. In fact, my own research shows that the word actually breaks down into two distinct parts—*Penta*, meaning "five," and *Ateuch* (pronounced "uh-TUCK") meaning "a tuck." Hence, *Pentateuch* means "five tucks."

Traditionally, the entire Pentateuch, including Genesis, is attributed to Moses. In a remarkable bit of authorship, Moses actually gives an account of his own death and burial in Deuteronomy 34:1–12. While many authors have continued to write long after their careers were dead, Moses is one of only a handful of writers who continued to write after they were actually dead—joining such legendary figures as James Michener and L. Ron Hubbard.

The books of the Pentateuch take us from creation to the end of the Mosaic era. The end of the Mosaic era came when humankind no longer made pictures primarily with small pieces of glass and stone, but rather began to explore other media such as photography and the internet.

The first two chapters of Genesis are concerned with the creation of the universe in six days, after which God rested. Because God is all-powerful, nobody really understands why He was tired after working for only six days. Some scholars believe that God wasn't tired, but that He simply wanted to watch a football game. In the Christian tradition, it is believed that the seventh day—the day of rest—fell on a Sunday. In the Jewish tradition, it is believed that the seventh day fell on a Saturday. To keep both sides happy and well rested, everyone decided that both Saturday and Sunday would be days of rest or weekends, with college football games being scheduled for Saturdays and professional football games scheduled for Sundays. God's preference for NFL over NCAA football remains a subject of debate to this day.

You may be interested to learn how the days of rest at the end of the week were named. (Note: This is the first of those hidden treasures we promised to reveal throughout the book.) It seems that everyone was so tired and weak from his or her five days of work that the week's end was marked by two days of rest called *weakened*.

I'm not making this stuff up. My pastor told me about the origin of the word *weekend*. My pastor is the man I most admire in the world. He's my spiritual advisor and the leader of a Presbyterian congregation in a small community in the western United States. Being a self-deprecating man, my pastor has asked me not to use his name in connection with this book. Austin says the real reason that my pastor doesn't want to be associated with this book is because he thinks I'm a nut. This is simply not the case. I have had many lengthy conversations, debates, and arguments with my pastor—the Reverend Alan Knudsen—over the spiritual issues and biblical facts that I will discuss in this book. These lively discussions have been extremely helpful in clarifying my beliefs. My pastor, always the joker, loves to play the devil's advocate by insisting that he disagrees with me on nearly every significant point we've ever debated. He has also suggested that I leave him alone and seek a new place of worship. It's this sense of humor that I find so compelling about the man.

I suppose that a discussion about the book of Genesis is also a good place to discuss in greater depth the genesis of this book. I didn't want to write it. Don't get me wrong, I'm fascinated with the subject matter and as a God-fearing man I felt I had something to say about it. The advance was tempting—well into the three figures. But I'm a busy guy. I had other fish that needed frying more urgently. Ultimately though, I decided I had to write this book for the benefit of Austin. I love him like the gerbil I never had. We've been collaborators since the late 1800s. He's a fine man, but (unlike me) Austin lacks spirituality in his life. I think even he would admit that he is envious of my deep faith and spirituality. I'm certain Austin wishes he were as pious and humble as I am. And it is because I am such a religious man that I have decided to cowrite this book with Austin in the hope that the experience of researching and writing a book about the Bible points him in the right direction.

That being said, let's get back to Genesis the book. What does the Bible say that God created on days one through six? Is the story credible? Although I'm a spiritual man, I'm also a questioning man. God gave us faith, but he also gave us a critical mind. We have the ability to reason. With that in mind, let's closely examine the creation story.

Day One

Genesis says that on the first day God created the heaven and the earth, and that He divided the day and the night. It says that just prior to this moment the land was formless and empty, dark all over and covered with water. So it existed before it existed. It's a paradox, but it's also quite simple to understand. It's like the chicken and the egg. And you can't create a universe without breaking a few eggs.

Day Two

On the second day God made the sky—a place for the sun, moon, stars, and birds. He also "made water above the sky."

This is an odd reference in Genesis. One can only presume that God considers the entire universe his own and, like a cosmic camper, He can make water anywhere He chooses (although I don't recommend doing it in poison ivy).

Let me make another observation at this point. For purposes of research, I have used the King James Bible. However, after months of work I happened upon a shocking fact. King James could not possibly have written the Bible. He succeeded Queen Elizabeth I as the monarch of Britain in the 1600s while all evidence indicates that the Bible was written between 1500 B.C. and A.D. 100. In addition to the obvious chronological discrepancy, there is a question of language. While the Bible was certainly written in English, there is little evidence that King James had the time or linguistic ability to write such a book. I will continue to look into this question. It may turn out to be the subject of my next book.

Day Three

God would like us to believe that He was extremely busy on Day Three, but don't believe it. He says He separated the water and the firmament and then created plant life. Other than the plant life, this sounds suspiciously like what God had been up to the previous day when he created a firmament in the midst of the waters to divide the waters from the waters. If the firmament dividing the waters was not land, then what was it? In my opinion, God kind of took it easy on Day Three. He made plants. Don't get me wrong. Plants are fantastic. It's just that God sort of padded his "Daily Report" when he says he also separated land from water on Day Three and tries to make it sound different from what He did on the previous day. Then again, maybe it took Him two days to separate water and land. This too is okay by me. Heck, I couldn't separate the water from the land in a thousand years. So maybe it took God two days to do it. And maybe He was embarrassed that He couldn't do it in the blink of an eye, so He listed this achievement over two days and tried to make it sound like two different things.

Very early texts refer to God's creation of television on the third day and his subsequent disappointment that cable service did not yet exist. For reasons never clearly understood, this portion of the creation story has been purged from later versions of Genesis.

Day Four

On Day Four, God gave a purpose to the lights He had created on the first day. They were to separate the day from the night, and to "mark seasons and days and years." It is not clear what the lights were doing during the two intervening days. As with Days Two and Three, what was created on Day Four sounds almost exactly like what was created on Day One. Maybe God took a day off on the fourth day, but denied it and made up some lame story about giving the lights a purpose. God continues to deny this accusation, but still looks awfully uncomfortable whenever the subject is raised.

In addition to the sun and the moon, Genesis says that God made the stars on Day Four. This shows how far back religion and celebrity have been intertwined. No wonder celebrities so often publicly thank God when they win an Oscar or a Super Bowl. He made them. That God created stars (or celebrities) on Day Four, but didn't make average human beings like Adam and Eve until Day Six speaks volumes. And it answers a question that has been on the minds of studio heads and sports executives for generations. Stars are made, not born.

Day Five

Living creatures of the sea and the sky were created on Day Five. This was an awful lot of work. Whether amphibians were created on this day or on Day Six, when creatures of the land were made, is unclear. Perhaps tadpoles were made on Day Five and frogs on Day Six. And I would not want to speculate on which day the platypus was created.

A brief side note to Day Five: Some people who call themselves Christians actually question whether the days of creation were literally twenty-four-hour periods. They speculate that the term *day* is figurative and that it refers to a much longer stretch of time. Let me be perfectly clear. The days referred to in the creation story were literally twenty-four-hour periods. People who deny this are not true Christians. They are the same sort of "Christians" who refer to the creation "myth." Creation is not a myth. It is a fact. I don't mean to be judgmental, but all of you who call these facts into question and propagate doubt among the faithful are going straight to hell. And, yes, hell literally exists. Have you ever been to New Jersey?

Day Six

On the sixth day, God created creatures that dwell on the land, as well as human beings—Adam and Eve.[1] God distinguished between humans and all other land-dwelling creatures, presumably because He knew that eventually humans would learn to fly and swim. And God gave humans dominion over all living creatures. I don't know why God gave humankind this responsibility, because as caretakers humans have left something to be desired. We have covered much of the earth with garbage and filled the sky with smoke. And those were just my cousins from Arkansas who live in the trailer park.

But seriously, in addition, many of God's original animals are now extinct. In retrospect, it may have been better for God not to put humans in charge but rather to let all creatures fend for themselves. Do not misunderstand me. God was not wrong. He is infallible. Let's just say that mistakes were made.

Without being specific, Genesis 1:26 says that God made

[1]Dinosaurs are not mentioned anywhere in the Bible. Fossil evidence is strong that they did actually exist. The best explanation that I have come up with for this apparent contradiction is that God placed the fossil evidence to test our faith. In other words, dinosaurs did not ever actually exist, but God placed phony fossil evidence in the ground to see how humans would react. (I didn't say it was a good explanation. I said it was the best explanation I could come up with.)

humans "after our likeness." This is more than a little disturbing. Does this mean we actually look like God? Does it mean we think like God? Does God lose His hair as He ages? Does He watch Jerry Springer when He's home in the afternoon? The mind races.

Day Seven

God orders a pizza and watches football, either college or professional depending on your faith. If the seventh day was a Saturday, God asks them to hold the bacon and pork sausage.

So there it is—an entire universe created in seven days. Not bad. Let me conclude this chapter with another "hidden treasure." It's not a hidden treasure from the Bible, but rather a theory that I've developed about creation. I think God made the whole universe in only one day. I know the Bible says that it took six days, but that's just an exaggeration by the liberal media. I think that God lazed around for five days, created everything on Day Six and then watched football on Day Seven. Because if humans were created in God's image, then God is a procrastinator too.

Chapter Two

Eat This

The Story of Adam and Eve
AUSTIN

Y ou think *your* family has problems? Adam and Eve are the original dysfunctional family. Maybe this is a comfort to you. I know it is to me.

It makes sense, doesn't it? Adam and Eve are the product of a broken home. They grew up without a strong maternal presence and with a stern Father who, at the first sign of disobedience, kicked them out of the house. They aren't *exactly* brother and sister, but they're still more intimately connected than mere strangers are. Eve is born of Adam's Rib, and Woman of the Year, and Guess Who's Coming to Dinner: she is Katherine Hepburn to Spencer Tracy's Adam.

Despite this closeness, Adam and Eve went forth and multiplied in defiance of contemporary society's more enlightened incest laws. The biological results were freakish and passed down to us in the form of vestigial baby toes, nipples on men, hairy women, and every seven generations a missing link: a man born with both a penis *and* a brain.

At first, everything was good. Adam's first assignment was to name the animals, and he nailed it. He got all of them right. (He was probably tired and confused by the time he got around to naming the seahorse and the butterfly, so we won't hold that against him.)

But his first disappointment came after he named all the dinosaurs. Even though they were only created on the fifth day, they were extinct by the end of the week. Adam goes to all the trouble of naming the dinosaurs and they go all extinct on him.[2]

But then God made for Adam a companion, whom he called Woman. That's when the trouble started.

Suddenly Adam notices long hair clogging up the river where he bathes.

Suddenly Adam's hearing about how he doesn't change his fig leaf often enough.

Suddenly Eve's complaining that they never talk anymore, even though they never talked at all prior to this and considering they haven't eaten from the tree of knowledge yet, don't have much to say.

Speaking of the tree of knowledge, God commanded Adam and Eve not to eat from this tree or they would die. This is just bad parenting. The minute you make something forbidden, you make it irresistible to a child. Admittedly, we get into some tricky theology here as God is generally referred to as "God the Father." He should really be called "God the Maker" (from the Yiddish word *macher*, meaning "really big cheese"). He's not a father in the classic biological sense because He never had sexual intercourse with anybody to beget a child. (You're thinking of Zeus, who was a totally different god altogether and who only had sex with mortal women while disguised as waterfowl.) Yes, there was that business with the Virgin Mary, but I don't think you could actually describe what happened there as sex. "Sex" is generally defined as "a consensual act between two adults, *both of whom notice what's happening and can remember it*" (emphasis added). I think if you asked Mary how she got pregnant (as I'm sure Joseph did repeatedly), she would tell you, sadly, that God was not much of a lover. She didn't even know

---

[2]With all due respect to Reed, this is the real reason dinosaurs aren't mentioned in the Bible. It'd just be rude to rub Adam's nose in the great dinosaur mishap.

he was there. That's our God. Omniscient, omnipotent, unnoticeable.

Anyway, God the Maker made the universe, the planets, and plants and animals and people. Now anybody with even a passing understanding of the Bible knows two things: God created a pristine paradise called Eden, and God is infallible. We get into some more tricky theology here with this idea of God's infallibility, because if God made any mistake (and I believe he made plenty), His creation of humans *has* to top the list. God gave Adam and Eve one simple rule: don't eat the fruit. Which is, of course, the *first* thing they did.

We also get into some tricky questions of feminism here, as Eve is depicted as disobedient, willful, and voracious. That's a whole 'nother story, and any publication entitled *Positive Images of Women in the Bible* would surely rank as one of the world's thinnest books. But I'd be excited to read any scholarly work that deals with disobedient, willful, and voracious biblical women. Especially in their underwear.

Sorry. Where were we? Right, the tree of knowledge.

Once they had both eaten the forbidden fruit, Adam and Eve were not ignorant innocents anymore. They had knowledge. Therefore, God had no choice—He *had* to kick them out of paradise. A mind is a terrible thing to use.

Adam and Eve's newfound knowledge led them to many discoveries. They discovered that Adam was from Mars and Eve was from Venus. They discovered their own shameful nakedness, after which they discovered that tab A fits nicely into slot B, allowing Eve to discover the incredibly painful beauty of childbirth. Then they jointly discovered the joys of parenting by giving birth to one beautiful boy and one jealous murderer. But even then, you can sort of understand where Cain was coming from. His daddy's the very first man in the world (gotta be tough to live up to *that*) and his mama's a naked thievin' former rib. Cain *has* to kill his own brother. It's the birth of the country-western song.

And it gets better. Adam and Eve have more sons and daughters, who then proceed to have even more sons and daughters—*with each other!* I'd be tempted to call them dirty and disgusting trailer trash if I didn't think I'd get irate letters from decent and hard-working trailer trash like Reed's cousins.

But this sort of sick inbreeding leads me back to the issue of God's infallibility. People who say God never makes mistakes ignore the Bible's most compelling evidence: God's own admission of guilt. God realized his mistake when he saw the deceitful immorality of humanity, and He said to Noah, "You know what? I screwed up." (I paraphrase.) "Humankind has filled my earth with evil and violence. I'm going to wipe everything out and start again." This is why Noah ends up building a huge boat in the middle of the desert.

But even after God destroyed every living creature with the flood of forty days and forty nights, humans continued to sin. They built towers up to God, they lied, they stole, they coveted, and they lay down with sheep (which is actually more of an "alternative lifestyle" and still quite popular in Wales, New Zealand, and certain parts of Montana). Jacob stole his brother's birthright, Joseph's brothers sold him into slavery, and the prophet Isaiah walked around naked for three years. It's the stuff of bad TV movies, which, come to think of it, are even further proof of God's questionable judgment.

But having said all that let me now say this: *I don't think it's all God's fault.*

I confess to a basic and profound personal dilemma here. I don't believe in God. I know it's odd that I should be cowriting a book about the Bible, but there it is.

What do I believe? I believe in ghosts. I believe in aliens. I believe in Bigfoot, the Loch Ness Monster, reincarnation, the love of family, the power of positive thinking, that the Chicago Cubs will one day win the World Series, and the Wonderbra.

But mostly I believe in Mark Twain, who wrote, "God created man in His image, and man, being a gentleman, returned the favor." The fact that ancient humanity imposed order on their chaotic world by creating the notion of a God much like themselves makes as much sense to me as the idea of an old guy with a beard sitting around who one day decides to spend a week creating all of creation.

You can see the jumble I'm in. I bet Reed doesn't struggle with this kind of self-doubt.[3]

Yes, the Bible is the Word of God. But it's written by man, and we know how unreliable men are. Men don't ask for directions. What makes you think they'll get the Word of God right?

The Bible is riddled with inconsistencies, but let me cite just one example. God saved Noah and his family because they were the only righteous and sober people on earth. Noah then proceeded to get hammered and pass out naked in his tent. Maybe I've been using the wrong definition of sober all these years.

Or maybe men wrote the Bible, men who are prone to getting things wrong.

It's a chicken-and-egg conundrum, no question. Is God such a lousy God that the best He can do is create an eternally fumbling and violent species like Homo sapiens? Or is God Himself the creation of a fumbling and violent species that only has the imagination to create a deity as fumbling and violent as itself? Who created whom here?

Maybe it's not God I don't believe in. Maybe I don't believe in Man.

I don't pretend to have the answers. But I sympathize with God, however real He is or isn't. Humankind—His creation—is a bunch of ungrateful deceitful children. I know what it's like because I'm a father myself. When Abraham finally agreed to make a covenant with Him, God ordered him to snip off the end of his penis to seal the deal. Ouch.

But I don't blame Him. I'd be angry too.

---

[3]Reed Martin here. The statements and mildly blasphemous utterings of Austin Tichenor in no way reflect the attitudes and/or belief systems of me, my family, the underwriters, or this publisher.

Chapter Three

Exodus!

Moses in the River
Moses in the Royal Family
Moses Leads the Exodus
Moses Is Refused Entry to the Promised Land
He Does Not Pass *Go.* He Does Not Collect $200

REED

Most biblical scholars consider the story of Moses a tale of triumph. I don't think so. Although Moses is considered the greatest of all biblical leaders, God does not allow Moses into the Promised Land. Why? Because Moses did not give all the credit to God for his great deeds.

And lest I be as guilty as Moses of taking credit from God, I'd like to apologize if I came off as holier-than-thou, or at least holier-than-Austin, in chapter 1. I don't think I'm better than Austin is, or if so, only slightly better. I'm no more a spiritual dynamo than any number of people—my pastor, Billy Graham, the pope. Anything I've accomplished in my life has been a blessing from God that I neither earned through my incredibly hard work nor deserved for my piety. If the last chapter is any indication, it does look like Austin now at least realizes that hell is a real possibility for him. I think this is the first step in his spiritual quest—the realization that maybe God exists. This is an answer to my prayers. I'd be overjoyed if Austin finds some spiritual insight as a direct result of my work with him on this book. And I'd give God all the credit.

19

The Story of Moses

When Moses is born, the Israelites have been living in Egypt for over four hundred years. The pharaoh is alarmed at the number and strength of the Hebrews, so he enslaves the Israelites. Though they are apparently not Catholics, the population of the Israelites continues to grow at an alarming rate. In lieu of birth control, Pharaoh orders the Hebrew midwives to kill all newborn Israelite males.

Enter Moses, born to Levite parents. Fearing for her son's life, Moses' mother does the only logical thing—she drops him into the Nile River. Today this would be considered child endangerment, but in those days it was considered good parenting. Moses' sister, Miriam, watches him float among the papyrus reeds until Pharaoh's daughter finds him. This princess adopts Moses.

Although raised in the Egyptian royal family, Moses is aware that he is a Hebrew. Without getting graphic, let's just say Moses realized he was missing a bit of skin at the end of one of his extremities. The inner conflict caused by his abandonment at an early age leads Moses to begin acting out. He becomes so infuriated when he witnesses an Egyptian beating a Hebrew that he kills the Egyptian. Fearing for his own safety, Moses flees Egypt to the Planet of the Apes. After being threatened by large, talking gorillas, he is befriended by two talking chimps—Kim Hunter and Roddy McDowell.

Moses falls in love with a beautiful woman who is unable to speak, and he becomes a shepherd. Let me clarify two things. First, Moses does not become a shepherd automatically when he falls in love with the mute beauty. It is just coincidence that they happen at about the same time. Second, there's an obvious joke to be made here about how every man fantasizes about being married to a beautiful woman who can't nag him, but I'm not even going to bring it up because it wouldn't be the Christian thing to do. Although I think I just did. And come to think of it, the Bible does teach that women should be submissive, so maybe mute women aren't such a bad idea. I'll have to ask my pastor about this. But in any case, Moses was the only human on the Planet of the Apes who wasn't mute. None of the other men or women could speak. And come to think of it, even the apes had trouble talking through those awkward gorilla masks.

Anyway, one day while grazing his sheep on Mount Sinai, Moses happens upon a horrifying vision from God—the Statue of Liberty on the beach. Though half destroyed in a nuclear war, Lady Liberty tells Moses he must go back to Egypt and free his people. Moses does not want to go, but is finally convinced when Lady Liberty promises him a cameo role in the sequel.

Upon returning to Egypt, Moses meets with Pharaoh and says, "Let my people go." Pharaoh refuses, so Moses calls on God to send plagues upon Egypt. The Nile River turns to blood. Frogs invade Egypt. Flies invade Egypt. Locusts invade Egypt. Finally, tourists invade Egypt. Still, Pharaoh is unmoved. Finally, God sends the ultimate plague on Pharaoh. He will be stuck performing *The King and I* for the rest of his life. This is too much for Pharaoh to bear. His spirit is broken and he tells Moses to get the Hebrews out of Egypt.

Quickly the Israelites gather their belongings and hit the road. They soon arrive at Universal Studios and witness the parting of the Red Sea on the back lot. Meanwhile, Pharaoh has changed his mind and orders his army to follow the Israelites. The Egyptians nearly catch the Hebrews, but are frightened off when the shark from *Jaws* attacks their tram. Heartbroken and humiliated, Pharaoh drops from sight for several years. Eventually he is cast as a robot cowboy in the film *Westworld* and then dies of lung cancer, but not before Moses' curse on Pharaoh comes to pass. He eventually does more than 10,000 performances of *The King and I*.

Meanwhile, the good news is that God's chosen people are finally free. The bad news is that they are stuck in the middle of the desert. After a period of celebration, the Israelites realize that life in the desert leaves something to be desired. They come to the conclusion that although being slaves in

Egypt wasn't fantastic, it sure beat the heck out of starving to death on the Sinai Peninsula. It's like the old joke about eating at a third-rate restaurant. The food is crappy, but at least there's plenty of it. Or maybe it wasn't like that old joke at all. You could make a case that conditions in the desert were crappy, but there was plenty of it. Or that certain things about being slaves were crappy, but that freedom's just another word for nothing left to lose.

I was getting a little confused about this whole line of thought, so I went to my pastor for counseling about it. He has a terrific sense of humor. I asked him what he thought the parallel might be between the old joke about eating at a third-rate restaurant and the Israelites wandering in the desert. I had repeated the old joke several times when he said he didn't understand why anyone would want to eat at a third-rate restaurant. He's such a kidder. I suggested that maybe the parallel was that in a restaurant you would eat *dessert*, while the Sinai Peninsula is a *desert*. He told me to get the heck out of his office. This was not the first *faux* rage he's directed at me over the last few months. I giggled all the way home.

In any case, Moses is facing mounting hostility from the Israelites stuck in the desert. Sensing that he's in deep trouble, Moses wonders whether he should face this problem head on or avoid it like a coward. He bravely chooses to run away to Mount Sinai.

On Mount Sinai, Moses again receives a message from God. Lady Liberty gives Moses two stone tablets that are inscribed with the Ten Commandments, also known as the Bill of Rights. The Ten Commandments are:

1. I am the Lord your God.
2. You shall have no other gods before me.
3. You shall not take the Lord's name in vain.
4. Remember the Sabbath Day and keep it holy.
5. Honor your father and your mother.
6. You shall not murder.
7. You shall not commit adultery.
8. You shall not steal.

9. You shall not lie.
10. You shall have the right to keep and bear arms.

Moses likes all the commandments, but especially the tenth. He believed that an armed citizenry is the cornerstone of democracy. But as soon as Moses comes down from the mountain and delivers the commandments to the people of Israel, he immediately encounters opposition led by his brother Aaron. Aaron points out to Moses that most other successful democracies, such as Canada and England, do not have armed citizens. Moses gets angry. Then Aaron asks him whether he thinks it makes sense that it would be easier for a citizen to get a gun license than a driver's license. Furious, Moses throws the commandments to the ground, shattering the tablets. He returns to Mount Sinai and God replaces the tablets, but this time God insists on a significant security deposit.

Moses comes back down from Mount Sinai and meets with Aaron. They agree to never again discuss politics or religion.

Eventually it comes time for God's chosen people to leave the foot of Mount Sinai. They follow a pillar of cloud by day and a pillar of fire by night through the desert. Priests carry the Ten Commandments in the ark of the covenant. Great care is taken in the handling of the ark of the covenant because Indiana Jones has warned Moses that Nazis are out to steal the ark and use it for diabolical purposes. The irony of anti-Semites attempting to steal the original Jewish laws is not lost on Moses. He starts to point out to Aaron that Hitler instituted gun control once he came to power and this greatly aided the ability of the Nazis to stifle their opposition. If ordinary German citizens had the right to bear arms they could have risen up and ousted Hitler. Aaron says using this sort of historical what-if in a debate is specious at best. Moses reasons that if guns are outlawed, then only outlaws will have guns. Then they remember that they have agreed not to discuss this topic anymore and they drop it.

The people of Israel have now been in the desert for over

a year. Although well tanned, they are getting hungry. God provides them with a mysterious food called manna. Nobody knows where it comes from, but it tastes a bit like chicken. Soon the people grow tired of having only one thing to eat, so God provides a second mysterious food—Soylent Green. Again nobody knows where it comes from, and it also tastes a bit like chicken.

The Hebrews spend forty years at an oasis in the desert, but eventually the water there dries up. The people grow discontented, not to mention thirsty. Moses asks God for help. God tells Moses to strike a rock with his staff and it will yield water. Moses does so and the people are amazed, but Moses fails to give God proper credit for this miracle. God is furious. And this is the great lesson—the hidden treasure, if you will—of the story of Moses: Give God the glory or you'll regret it. God and Moses submit to binding arbitration with the Screen Writers' Guild over the issue of proper credit. They rule that God should get full credit and, as punishment for horning in on God's glory, Moses will not be allowed to enter the Promised Land. He will, however, get a two-picture deal with Universal.

Chapter Four

Hollywood and Divine

The History Books

AUSTIN

The next nine books—Joshua, Judges, Ruth, Samuel, Kings, Chronicles, Ezra, Nehemiah, and Esther—represent the "historical" section of the Bible. They depict the rise and fall and rise again of Israel. Sounds pretty dry, right? Happily, this is not the case. The authors of these books knew how to spice up even the dullest history lesson with sex.

With all due respect, I think Reed's admirable but childlike faith has done him a disservice. Is it me, or did Reed just confuse the story of Moses with the film career of Charlton Heston? Maybe it's a bit of biblical pedagogy I'm unfamiliar with, but as it stands now, I'd have to say that Reed's interpretation of Exodus is historically flawed and intellectually simpleminded. Nonetheless, it's intriguing (but don't forget—it's also flawed and simpleminded).

It's intriguing because Reed's subconscious (or is it unconscious?) has led him to make an inspired connection between the Bible and Hollywood. Hollywood, after all, is now the scapegoat-du-jour for whatever's ailing American society. Whether it's the decline of morals, the rise of violence, the lowering of standards, the loss of innocence, the drop in attendance, the lapse of taste, the depression of the economy, the petering-out of potency, the fall of humanity, the wages of sin, the lack of attention, the merchant of Venice, the bridge too far, or the inevitable expiration of effective examples, Hollywood is to blame. Like Hollywood screenwriters who never get the credit if a movie is good, Hollywood always gets the blame when society goes bad.

But no one ever asks the most important question: What is to blame for Hollywood?

The answer is clear—the Bible.

Mission: Implausible

The Bible's pernicious influence can be traced directly to the book of Joshua, a sanitized, idealized, almost Hollywood-ized account of the conquest of Canaan. The story introduces us to Joshua ben Jerry, a military aide to Moses and maker of ice cream. Joshua sends two spies to scout the border town of Jericho. Once inside, they meet the woman who is the model for a classic Hollywood archetype—Rahab, the famous "hooker with a heart of gold."

Rahab allows the two spies to spend the night with her. The Bible discreetly declines to offer details but the implication is clear—there were hot times in the old town that night. Rahab, being an enterprising businesswoman, offers to help the spies escape if they in turn promise to protect her and her family from the coming invasion. Rahab probably offers more mattress-dancing to sweeten the deal, a sort of *quim pro quo* that was a standard biblical transaction. This is a better use of sex than in most Hollywood movies, which can't be bothered to find a real reason for sex and nudity so simply resort to gratuitous displays of topless women.[4]

But now the story gets taken over by Hollywood special-effect trickery. First, a blast of trumpets brings the walls of Jericho tumbling down. Then the River Jordan parts exactly like the Red Sea parted, allowing the Israelites to enter the

---

[4]Not that there's anything wrong with that.

Promised Land in high style. Once the river stands dry, it stops being the River Jordan and becomes the Air Jordan, a biblical brand name that soon dominates Israeli advertising. Water parting quickly becomes a Bible cliché. Soon every tiny puddle gets parted just because it can, just like how in every movie nowadays the hero has to outrun a flaming ball of fire.

And in the greatest special effect of all, the sun and the moon stop in the sky. They hang there, frozen, allowing Joshua and his troops to win the battle. The enemy turns and runs, but because it is a biblical and Hollywood tradition that the bad guy is never *really* dead, just as they are about to regroup and attack again, they're killed by a humongous hailstorm. Another victory for God, and for over-the-top special effects.

Much of the story of Joshua plays like a replay of the Moses story, which is exactly the reason why Hollywood gets its love of sequels from the Bible. Why do you think the text that's used as a blueprint for making movies is called a *script*? Because it's short for *scripture*. When people talk about "the Bible of the industry," they're usually referring to *Variety* or *The Hollywood Reporter*.[5] Really, the Bible of the industry is the Bible.

In the final dénouement, Joshua divides up the conquered land into twelve areas, one for each of the twelve tribes of Israel. (Instead of being given any actual land, the tribe of Levi is ordered to serve the priesthood and design and develop a line of denim trousers.) The tribes are even given land they don't actually possess, much like the current Hollywood practice of awarding "net points," meaning a percentage of the profits, to some of its creative personnel. The joke is that due to some even more creative accounting, there are no net points. Hollywood movies never actually make a profit. Art Buchwald and the author of *Forrest Gump* know exactly how the twelve tribes of Israel feel.

---

[5]Although it's actually *TV Guide*.

Twelve Angry Tribes

And yet, rather than tell any of the dozen or so stories that suggest themselves at the end of Joshua, what does the Bible do? *It tells the same story again.*

The book of Judges is a different version of the same material found in Joshua. It's messy, unflattering, and out of focus—the indie film version of the Hollywood blockbuster we've already seen. *The Blair Witch Project* to Joshua's *Sixth Sense*. Joshua with street cred.

In fact, Joshua and Judges are two examples of the Bible's greatest achievement, which is this: *the Bible offers something for everyone.* Like the weather in New England, if you don't like something in the Bible, just wait. An alternate version—or something altogether contradictory—will come along very soon. This has to be God's way of recognizing the many different people of the world. God knows (since He's omniscient) that people have different tastes and don't always enjoy the same things. So He acknowledges, tolerates, and more importantly, *provides for* alternative tastes and lifestyles. Unfortunately, He chose not to pass on this understanding and tolerance to religious zealots, the ones who put the *mental* in *fundamentalist.*

In fact, Hollywood should try to follow the Bible's example here too. Make movies for *everyone*, not just for teenagers. How about a movie where a bespectacled curly-headed middle-aged scholar, with a keen mind and keener wit, wins the love of a gorgeous and intelligent grad student who caters to his every sexual whim while he fills her mind with intelligence and insight?[6]

Judges isn't slick. On a plot level, it's pretty repetitive: the Israelites prosper, stop worshiping, get punished, cry for help, and are judged—repeatedly. But it still has the same elements of sex and violence that God and Hollywood love so well.

First is the judge Deborah, "blessed above women" for being a prophet and a butt-kicking, battle-leading babe. She

[6]Oh, never mind. They make plenty of those kinds of movies already.

has that combination of sex appeal and military strength that won't be seen again until Pamela Lee Anderson.

A Star Is Shorn

Then comes the story of Samson, a one-man army who hates the Philistines for killing his bride and burning her body. (Alert readers will recognize this as the inspiration for the movie *Braveheart*, which included such accurate details as Samson's blue face paint and the bum-flashing, kilt-wearing Hebrews.) Samson single-handedly slaughters thousands of Philistines using nothing but the jawbone of Jesse Helms. God gives Samson his remarkable strength in exchange for a single vow—never to cut his hair. This biblical Fabio falls in love with the treacherous Delilah, who betrays him and cuts off his hair while he sleeps. Delilah's pretty tough, but when it comes to cutting, she doesn't come close to Lorena Bobbitt. And really—a hero whose strength is in his *hair?* Even *Batman* at its campiest never tried something that lame. I'd have to give this one a thumbs-down.

Samson is captured, has his eyes gouged out, is paraded as a war trophy, and is tied to two pillars. By this time his hair has grown out, and with the standard battle cry ("This time, it's personal!") Samson brings the temple crashing down on his enemies and himself.

If that weren't enough fun, some men from the tribe of Benjamin gang rape a woman to death. Then the husband cuts up her body and sends the eleven pieces to the other eleven tribes. (Explain to me again why we encourage children to read the Bible. This stuff is *horrible*.) A bloody civil war ensues, all but destroying the tribe of Benjamin. This lovely ultraviolence inspires the late Stanley Kubrick to have the Bible banned in England. Sadly, he is unsuccessful and the Bible's violent influence continues unchecked.

Sex and the Walled City

The Book of Ruth contains a different kind of moral lesson. It's the classic Hollywood story of a woman who sleeps her way to the top. Thematically, it's the story of her salvation, how even an outsider, a non-Jew, can choose God and find redemption, blah blah blah. What *really* happens is this: Ruth finds salvation through premarital sex. (I take it back. This is *great* for kids!)

One night, after enduring much hardship, which includes losing her husband, Ruth crawls into the bed of Boaz, a relative or in-law of some kind. Boaz wakes up, feels what is happening under his covers and exclaims, "Blessed be!" (Ruth 3:10. In the same situation, I once said something very similar.) Boaz, however, takes the next step and agrees to marry her because he's so impressed by her loyalty to her family and Jewish tradition. Yeah, me too.

Now get this: despite the somewhat scandalous origins of their relationship, Ruth and Boaz ultimately give birth to Obed, who becomes the grandfather and great-grandfather of the great kings of Israel, David and Solomon.

Now get *this:* David and Solomon, descendants of this unorthodox couple, are ancestors of *Jesus Christ himself.*

So were you paying attention? This is another hidden treasure we promised you in the introduction. Remember Rahab, the hooker with the heart of gold? She was Boaz's *mother!* That's right—Jesus is directly descended from a prostitute.

I am not making this up. No wonder Jesus felt so comfortable around Mary Magdalene. She was like one of the family.

Is this the reason Americans have such a confused attitude towards prostitution? You'd think apocalyptic fundamentalists would be *rushing* to prostitutes in hopes of giving birth to a new messiah and hurrying along the Second (you'll pardon the expression) Coming. This could very well explain the behavior of people like Jimmy Swaggart. On the other hand, maybe that's why so many people dislike the idea of prostitution. One messiah was enough, thank you very much.

Anyway, moving on.

Three Faces of Samuel

The books of Samuel, Kings, and Chronicles are each broken in two, so we have 1 Samuel and 2 Samuel, 1 Kings and

2 Kings, and so on. Supposedly, this was to make the separate books fit onto one scroll and therefore be easier to carry. But really it's that old Hollywood trick of making two movies out of one story and doubling the return on your investment (see *The Three/Four Musketeers, Back to the Future Two/Three, The Matrix II/III*, and *Rocky One through Seventeen*).

Samuel is a prophet, and the books named for him celebrate the good life—wenching, debauchery, music, and killing. Basically, they're party books. It's interesting to note that the word *prophet* comes from the Greek words meaning "to speak forth," that is, to relate and interpret the will of God as revealed in a trance or ecstasy, often of the chemically induced variety. First Samuel 10:10 describes "a company of prophets" who play instruments, sing, dance, fall down in a frenzy, and put themselves into wild trances. Sounds like any random fraternity party on a Friday night. In college I remember speaking to the Big Guy on a regular basis, so Samuel speaks to me on a deeply personal level.

On the mundane plot level, though, the Samuels tell the history of Israel when it changed from twelve independent tribes into one nation ruled by a single king. But oh! The subtext reveals a deeper and more disturbing truth, which is this God and Hollywood love beautiful people best of all.

We've seen it before with Jacob's preference for the beautiful Rachel over the plain-but-fertile Leah. Samuel, in his role of kingmaker, chooses a couple of pretty-boys. Saul is described in 1 Samuel 9:2 as "a choice young man, and a goodly . . . from his shoulders and upward he was higher than any of the people" (meaning he was taller, not that he had smoked more dope than Cheech and Chong). But anyway, we get it. He's a stud.

Depending on which Bible you read, David was either "ruddy, and . . . beautiful . . . and goodly to look to" (1 Samuel 16:12, King James Version), or in the words of my New Revised Contemporary Translation, a "smokin' hottie." No mention of wit or wisdom—like presidential elections and Hollywood casting sessions, it's a beauty contest all the way. I'm surprised Samuel didn't outline a detailed beauty regimen with specific techniques for waxing hairy eyebrows or tightening flabby buttocks (the latter, of course, being the origin for Jesus' famous admonition to "firm the other cheek").

Better than all of this is that Samuel gives us a—hidden treasure alert!—*glimpse into the mind of God.* David is described in 1 Samuel 13:14 as "a man after [God's] own heart." That's right. The same David who slaughters the male descendants of his vanquished opponents, spies on naked Bathsheba while she's bathing, invites her to the palace, gets her pregnant, kills her husband, and marries her—turns out this is God's kinda guy. David's a hero and a great king, but he's got a dark side. He's clearly the inspiration for the Hollywood antihero, and why they cast Richard Gere in the movie I'll never understand. Harvey Keitel would have been better.

Anyway, it's good to know that the man after God's own heart is a violent, promiscuous Peeping Tom. Makes my own life seem like such a waste.

David does get the Hollywood gloss-over, though. In 1 Samuel 16:23, he's described as a harpist, then in the very next chapter he's introduced a second time as the winner of the famous battle with Goliath. First he's a musician, then he's a military hero, much like Daryl Hannah in *Roxanne*, in which she plays a brilliant astronomer (you know she's brilliant because she wears glasses) but is also a babe. That's the Bible I love—something for everyone.

I Know What You Did Last Rosh Hashanah

But God doesn't always let rampant sex go unpunished. Kings 1 and 2 read like a typical horror movie, where the horny teens are slaughtered by a deranged serial killer. Only in this case, the Jews are the horny teens and God is the deranged serial killer.

Wise old King Solomon had 700 royal wives and 300 concubines. Not surprisingly, the demands of a thousand women are fairly exhausting. It's amazing Solomon could stand up, let alone serve the Lord like he was supposed to.

And if that's not bad enough, the famous floozy Jezebel appears. She's married to King Ahab, one of the ungodly kings of the northern nation of Israel, which was divided along a sort of Jewish Mason-Dixon line by God as punishment for Solomon's fornication—it's a long story. The point is, Jezebel thinks Ahab's a loser because he's weak and has a thing for whales, so she begins executing God's prophets (which should not be confused with Jim Bakker's *PTL Club*, which are God's *profits*) and imposing her own religion on the nation. Jezebel worshiped Baal, a fertility god who demanded such tribute as having sex with both men and women. Maybe God got up on the wrong side of heaven that day because, frankly, Jezebel sounds like a woman after His own heart. Nonetheless, God destroys Israel as punishment. Again.

Intermission

Then, just like intermission in a long movie, comes a little breather. Chronicles recaps everything we've learned up to now, like a TV announcer saying, "Previously, in *The Bible* . . ." or a new chapter in a serialized novel beginning "The story so far . . ."

The theological purpose of this summation is to let the Jews know that, yes, they screwed up, but they are still God's Chosen People. (At which point, it wouldn't have been inappropriate to hear the Jews rise as one and say, quoting Tevye the milkman, "Couldn't you for once choose somebody *else?*") God wants the Jews to know He hasn't forgotten about them, or their history. Basically, He's setting up those poor Semitic suckers for another fall.

Indiana Jones and the Temple of Solomon

The Book of Ezra is like the classic Hollywood movie that doesn't know what it wants to be. It depicts the rise (once again) of Israel, but it also slyly insinuates that there may be room in the world for other ideologies. Although the priest Ezra preaches that Jews should never marry non-Jews, we also see three pagan kings help rebuild Solomon's Temple. We can also remember the story of Ruth, the famous non-Jew redeemed by her marriage into the faith. But on the other hand, if we remember that Ruth's descendant, that famous Jew, Jesus of Nazareth, became that even more famous non-Jew, Jesus Christ, we can maybe see Ezra's point. Ezra would be more than justified if he pointed at the rise of Christianity and said, "See? I told you there'd be trouble."

But Nehemiah! There's an awesome book! I give it four stars, two thumbs up! Nehemiah, a servant to the king, despairs that the walls of Jerusalem have been torn down and decides to rebuild them—all by himself! Well, not all by himself, but he oversees the project and it's completed in an amazing fifty-two days.

Can you not immediately picture this as a great role for Harrison Ford? Especially given his well-known passion for carpentry? Nehemiah is a stud (no pun intended), the Israelite version of Da Man! (No pun even remotely implied.) And, although he's devoutly religious and prays regularly, he doesn't sit around waiting for God to do the work. Despite objections and attacks and threats, Nehemiah gets the job done. He's a hero, plain and simple. Actually, if he's played by Harrison Ford, he's a hero, rugged and intense.

Nehemiah's achievement seems even more remarkable when we realize that as a palace servant who worked in the presence of the queen, he was probably a eunuch. Ouch! No wonder he had so much time on his hands. Yet despite the absence of his Jewish jewels, he still erects the massive walls of Jerusalem. As Sigmund Freud might have said, "Compensate much?"[7]

---

[7]In fact, William Shakespeare wrote one of his greatest works about Nehemiah's achievement, calling it *Much Ado Without Something*.

Esther Parade

The Bible's something-for-everyone policy continues with the book of Esther. The story of a strong male hero (admittedly, a hero without those two special doodads that make him male) is followed by a story of a strong female hero who basically saves the Jews from a holocaust. It's a good story but I'm not going to retell it here. Read it yourself. Seriously, go do it. It's a fun story. It's also kind of moving. The plot hinges on some fairly amazing coincidences, but still, it's pretty enjoyable. Another plus? Esther is one of the shortest books in the Old Testament. You can read the whole thing on your next trip to the bathroom. It's also the basis for the Jewish festival of Purim, which, admittedly, is way up there in the Who Cares? Department but is still fun to know.

Also fun to know is the fact that the book of Esther is the one book in the entire Bible in which the word *God* does not appear. Not once. Many scholars argue that even though God does not make an appearance, His work can be seen in the unlikely string of coincidences that I've already mentioned, as well as the many leaps of storytelling logic.

Unlikely coincidences? Leaps of logic? That's not God's work. That's bad writing. By that measure, the book you're reading right now is the most divine work ever created.

Home Alone X: The Epiphany

But still, Esther hits very close to home. My home.

Ironically, this absence of God served as a personal smack in the face, in the same way my wife's reaction to my intensive research into the early biblical influences of Uma Thurman and Heather Graham served as an actually painful nonmetaphorical smack in the face. In the midst of researching the Esther section, I was struck (in the metaphorical, nonspousal way) by the fact that I, too, don't have the word *God* appearing anywhere in my life. I've written earlier about my agnostic struggle with my beliefs. But the book of Esther inspired me to do something about it.

My own upbringing was in the devoutly Christian tradition of never setting foot inside a church except for weddings and funerals. I was never baptized, although my parents were: one as an Episcopalian, the other as a Methodist, but it would take a deeper theological thinker than I to tell you the difference between the two.[8]

When I was very young we would read aloud the stories of Jesus' birth and resurrection on Christmas and Easter mornings. We stopped reading about Jesus around the same time I discovered the truth about Santa Claus and the Easter Bunny. Somehow it seemed silly and childish to believe in Jesus after realizing the stories of Santa and the Bunny made more sense.

But until I read Esther, I never considered what I was missing. Not until God was so conspicuous by His absence in Esther did I realize there was a vast emptiness in my own soul as well. I decided to explore, to attain that special feeling, that deep serenity which can only be achieved by accepting that tell-me-anything-and-I'll-believe-it-no-matter-how-ridiculous-it-sounds thing called *faith*.

Earlier I admitted that I didn't believe in God. It's probably more accurate to say that I do believe in God—I just don't believe in religion. Religion has often been referred to as a crutch, but I think it's more like a club: a club that gives its members both a sense of belonging and exclusivity, and pounds in the idea that membership guarantees superiority over other, lesser clubs. I mean religions.

But maybe I wasn't being fair. So I began to look around.

I considered converting to Judaism since I had always been a big fan of Sammy Davis Jr. and thought that converting had sure worked for him. Also, I get asked if I'm Jewish a lot. I don't know why. Could be my curly-headed, glasses-wearing, self-deprecating wit. Could be because I'm tight with a buck. Hard to tell.

---

[8]Between the two religions, I mean. It was almost always pretty easy to tell my mother and father apart. Mom was the one with the curly hair who laughed at my jokes. I grew up thinking I got my sense of humor from my dad because my mom still had hers.

But I decided against it. Even though I could have saved money on the *bris*, it just didn't seem right to me. Being Jewish is as much cultural as it is religious, and despite my affection for that great Talmudic scholar Dr. Laura, I just didn't feel I had enough *chutzpah* to go through with it.

I've always had a special fondness for Islam because I love Cat Stevens and think Salman Rushdie is overrated. Plus, Muslims have contributed more to world culture than they ever get credit for (such as algebra and coffee to name just two) and are, generally speaking, the most easygoing and tolerant people in the world. The Hollywood stereotype of Muslims is unfortunate and completely unfounded. Great gangs of Muslims never demonstrate in the streets against the "Great Satan," nor has any Muslim ever blown up a building or hijacked a plane. Muslims, unlike members of other religions, are perfect. In fact, I don't think it's going too far to say that Islam deserves the rank of World's Greatest Religion.

But it's not for me. One, I'm just too damn lazy. There's no way I could ever pray that many times a day. Plus, I have a terrible sense of direction. I can just see myself bowing down, facing southwest, and bringing a *jihad* down on my head.

Hinduism has always appealed to me. It has very little organization and no hierarchy, which is cool and remarkably similar to the Democratic Party. Its notion of *karma* is a powerful one, a system of checks and balances for the here and now. Like whenever my travel *karma* is good, when the lights are all green and there's always an available parking space, it's almost always because I've been a very good guy the day before. I prefer the immediacy of these little rewards to the ultimate promise of heaven or hell in exchange for a *lifetime* of behavior. Gee, could Christianity apply *more* pressure?

But no. Can't do the Hindu thing. No real reason, either. Well, no good reason. Tell you the truth, I'm crazy about cheeseburgers.

Buddhism, again, is like a lifestyle choice I'm too lazy to

make. Despite my fondness for both Winnie the Pooh and Phil Jackson, I'm just too old to bend my legs into that chanting position. Buddhism's a young man's game.

I love the Mormons, particularly since they dropped that thing about the special underwear. And have you seen Mormon women? Jesus Christ, they're beautiful.[9] But I was in Salt Lake City one Christmas and saw all the beautiful Mormons milling around. I swear to God, it was like being in the *Village of the Damned*. Or the *Children of the Corn*. What's the one with the blond, vacant-eyed children? Anyway, that one. Plus, I don't really trust a religion whose founder uses such an obvious alias as "Joe Smith." On top of that, they now prohibit polygamy, and I'm *really* not crazy about tithing. It's bad enough giving ten percent of your income to your agent. Giving ten percent to your religion just seems gauche, like slipping Saint Peter an extra sawbuck to get a table closer to God.[10]

Speaking of tithing, I decided to check into Scientology. I know, a lot of people think Scientology should be called a cult rather than a religion, but I think that's unfair. Because really, what *is* a religion anyway except a cult with legs? As far as I can tell, Scientology doesn't require self-mutilation like circumcision or the ingestion of harmful beverages like spiked Kool-Aid and sacramental wine. But still, in places like Germany, Scientologists are required to have a stamp on their passports identifying them, and they're forbidden to own businesses. They're plucky though, these Scientologists. Their brochures are emblazoned with their new slogan: "Check us out! We're the new Jews!"

Since I live in Los Angeles it was simplicity itself to check into the fastest growing religion in show business. Here's what I found out. Scientology apparently teaches that aliens called "thetans" visited Earth about 70,000 years ago. These

---

[9]I'm not taking Jesus' name in vain here, so don't write letters. I'm telling my buddy, Jesus Christ, about the aesthetic attributes of the female Latter-day Saints.

[10]I don't even want to talk about Donny and Marie. A divorced Mormon? Come on.

thetans are immortal spirits who reside inside each one of us, manifesting themselves as past painful experiences, or "engrams," in our unconscious, or "reactive" mind. The goal of Scientology is to rid the thetans of these negative influences through a ritual known as auditing, which increases one's spiritual awareness and abilities. One is cleansed with a machine called an "E-meter," which aids in the auditing process. And apparently, devout Scientologists must forgo all other forms of therapy, beginning with psychoanalysis and including everything up to massage and presumably even getting their nails done, in order to completely rid themselves of the alien thetans and achieve their ultimate potential.

Well, that's ridiculous.

You call this a religion? Aliens? E-meters? I can't take all this science fiction mumbo jumbo in a religion. Give me something I can sink my teeth into, something real and verifiable, like that religion where the descendant of a prostitute is born unto a virgin apparently impregnated by an alien spirit, and who dies but then springs back to life, and then flies up into heaven. Now *that* makes sense.

On the other hand, Scientology claims as its victims—sorry, members—people like John Travolta and Tom Cruise, both of whom are incredibly talented and successful and, more importantly, married to desperately beautiful women. So Scientology must be doing something right.

Because as we've seen in the Bible, that Hollywood connection is extremely important.

Roll credits.

Chapter Five

The Brighter Side
of Job and Lamentations

REED

You wouldn't think a book called Lamentations would be very funny, but you would be wrong. The story of Job is sad and depressing, but can also be quite amusing if you look at it the right way. The hidden treasure of Lamentations and Job is that they are actually carefully constructed comic masterpieces.

Lamentations

The book of Lamentations is an anonymous work traditionally attributed to Jeremiah and consists of five carefully constructed dirges or poems. Dating from about 586 B.C., it laments the destruction of Jerusalem by Nebuchadnezzar of Babylon.

The most famous of the dirges is the fifth. It includes the famous line, "There once was a heathen from Nantucket. . . ."

Under the guise of mourning the dead, Jeremiah spends the entire book kvetching. Nothing makes him happy. Everything is wrong. He goes on and on about seemingly nothing at all. Jeremiah was the *Seinfeld* of his day.

Chapter 1

Jeremiah finds a lot of humor in complaining about the recent flight of the Israelites from Jerusalem. He is whining with good reason. Flights in those days were just awful. First of all, there were no planes. This was a big problem. People had to take flight by foot or by camel. There were no in-flight meals or movies. And you were not allowed to check any bags. All baggage was carry on.

Toward the end of chapter 1 Jeremiah finds some positives in taking flight without a plane. There is plenty of leg room in the desert. The air is not recycled. The stewardesses are not old and grumpy. Heck, there aren't any stewardesses.

He concludes the first dirge with the observation that although it's hard to get a drink in the desert, it's just as hard to get a drink when you fly economy.

Chapter 2

By the second chapter, Jeremiah has realized that the Israelites themselves and not the Babylonians are to blame for their bad fortune. They have brought on their own trou-bles. If they had followed the rules, everything would have been fine. But they took a couple of envelopes home from the office. They ate a little bit of granola from the bulk bin at the supermarket without paying for it. They watched *Geraldo*. They thought nobody knew. But God knew.

In Lamentations 2:11 Jeremiah notes, "My bowels are troubled, my liver is poured upon the earth." This is a specific reference to the quality of the food in the Middle East 2500 years ago. In short, it was terrible. Meals in those days made British food seem like haute cuisine. Fresh pro-duce was almost impossible to find in the middle of the desert. Seasonings (other than salt and sun-dried tomatoes) were virtually nonexistent. In any case, this bad diet appar-ently gave Jeremiah "troubled bowels." The situation came to a head one Sunday when his wife prepared liver and onions for dinner. Jeremiah hated liver and his wife knew it, but it was all she had in the fridge and all the markets in the desert were closed on Sundays. Furious, Jeremiah dumped his liver and onion dinner "upon the earth." His wife gave him the silent treatment all the way to Egypt.

Chapter 3

Jeremiah observes that all Babylonians are bad drivers. They put on their turn indicators after they have already started to turn their camels. They don't bring their camels to a complete standstill at stop signs, but just sort of slow down and then continue on in what has come to be termed a rolling "Babylonian stop." Worst of all, they tailgate. Jeremiah wasn't afraid that his camel would be rear-ended. Heck, camels can stop on a shekel. But he knew that good drivers keep a distance of at least four camels between themselves and the next dromedary. Four body lengths happens to be the spitting range of the average camel.

Jeremiah reads the ancient laws for amusement. One obscure statute forbids throwing a lighted cigarette from a moving camel. He says, "What are they afraid of? Do they think they're going to light the desert on fire?"

Eventually Jeremiah comes to understand that the Hebrews' punishment will not go on forever. God is going to give them a break. They will have the opportunity to go to Comedy Camel Traffic School. They will not learn anything useful there, but God will clear their camel driving record and lower their insurance rates.

Chapter 4

The whole mood of Lamentations shifts in chapter 4. Jeremiah's humor becomes dark and surreal. One of the funniest verses in the entire Old Testament is Lamentations 4:3. It is as funny today as when it was written. Jeremiah simply says, "Even the sea monsters draw out the breast, they give suck to their young ones: the daughter of my people is become cruel, like the ostriches in the wilderness." That ostrich part tickles me every time I read it.

Chapter 5

The final chapter is a prayer that acknowledges sin as the reason that the Israelites are currently in a bad way. Jeremiah asks God to restore and renew his people. Deep down there is a sense of faith in God and a belief that things will get better. It is with this background that Jeremiah lightheartedly pokes fun at the young people of the time—the future leaders of Israel.

Jeremiah says that their music isn't really music. It is too loud. And what's with this big hit "Hava Nagila"? The lyrics are indecipherable. You'd think they were singing in a foreign language or something.

Jeremiah points out that the kids are lazy and reminds everyone that he had to walk to school seven miles each way, barefoot in the freezing snow. This is something of an exaggeration since there is no record of it ever having snowed in the Sinai Desert during Jeremiah's lifetime. He laments the fact that the kids don't appreciate their school supplies because they are provided for free. In Jeremiah's day he had to buy his own school tablets and papyrus.

Jeremiah concludes his lamentations on an optimistic note. He acknowledges that he is just a grumpy old codger, and that everything is going to turn out just fine. Now if only those sheep next door would stop bleating all night long.

At this point my pastor has asked me to make a disclaimer. We have discussed my views and he says my take on Lamentations has little, if any, connection whatsoever with the biblical book. He's pulling my leg again. I did have a small computer glitch while researching the book of Lamentations, but I got it sorted out. My Lamentations file was temporarily corrupted by a CD-ROM I was using, "Milton Berle's Guide to Comedy." I was trying to find a few jokes to cheer up my pastor when the glitch occurred. He has been on a personal leave of absence from the church for a couple of weeks now, trying to sort out a bout of depression. He wasn't home when I went over to drop off the jokes, which was odd because his car was in the driveway and his TV was on. Anyway, the front door was unlocked (also odd), so I took the liberty of going into his office. I left a printout of several jokes by Milton Berle on top of the book he's reading—*How to Deal with Difficult People*. I hope they cheer him up.

Job

Job is funny. Really funny. It's the biblical equivalent of the TV show *America's Funniest Workplace Dismemberments*. Terrible things happen to Job, but ultimately everything turns out okay. We can laugh because we know in the end that no human beings were actually killed during filming. Except for Job's family. But we're getting ahead of ourselves.

The book of Job appears almost exactly halfway through the Bible and is apparently placed there as a sort of ice breaker just before Psalms and Proverbs, in the same way that a speaker will often open with a joke before getting into a lengthy speech.[11]

Originally Austin was going to write this chapter. But I decided that Job would be a bad book for Austin to read at this point in his spiritual walk. That's why I told him that I'd cover it. Job is a book intended for someone with a mature faith in God. The God that tests Job is the vengeful, Old Testament God. Our loving New Testament God of today doesn't work that way. Much. But Austin might just read Job and decide that a life with God is about as enjoyable as a root canal.

Job is a wealthy, righteous, and devoted servant of God. As a reward for being so faithful, God allows terrible things to happen to Job. Who says God doesn't have a sense of humor?

You see, Satan and God got into a friendly little discussion that led to Job's troubles. Satan tells God that Job is only faithful because he's healthy, wealthy, and happy. Satan says that if Job suffers a little bit, he'll fall away from God. God says, "No way." Satan says, "Way." God says, "No way." Satan says, "Way." They go on like this for what seems an eternity (maybe it actually *was* an eternity) when they agree

---

[11]A good source for an opening joke is "Milton Berle's Guide to Comedy."

that the only way to find out is to have a little fun with Job. And, indeed, Job ends up having very little fun. In fact, he has become a symbol for all those who endure endless suffering for no reason—like Los Angeles Clippers fans.

Job's problems begin slowly. First, Satan short-sheets his bed. Job laughs it off. Then Satan phones him, asking him if his refrigerator is running. Job takes it in stride. Satan knocks at Job's door and then runs away before Job can answer. Job is still nonplussed and Satan comes to the conclusion that he's going to have to take out the heavy artillery if he's going to break Job's spirit.

Satan arranges to have raiders steal Job's flocks and murder his servants, but then has second thoughts. Satan decides to try one last, less severe practical joke. He sets a bag of doggy droppings on Job's doorstep and lights it on fire. He rings the doorbell and dashes away. Job comes to the door, stomps out the fire and ends up with a soiled shoe. And, unfortunately, he takes the whole thing in his characteristic good humor. The next thing Job knows, his herds are gone and his servants are dead. He has essentially been punished more harshly for being good-natured. Nice one, God.

Next, Satan arranges for a windstorm to crush the house where Job's children are eating. They are all killed. Job screams at God. He wants to know why this is happening. Though Job has not yet lost faith, he has now lost his cool. Satan feels on the verge of proving his point. Having taken away Job's wealth and family, Satan targets his health. Job breaks out in skin ulcers. His body is covered in open, festering sores. Now Satan can see that both Job's skin and spirit are beginning to crack.

And speaking of someone who's beginning to crack, I just ran into my pastor, the Reverend Alan Knudsen, at Jumbo Discount Liquors. I was taking a break from writing and went out to get a Jolt Cola and some deep-fried pork rinds. I asked Reverend Alan if my jokes had cheered him up, but he just mumbled something unintelligible and kept walking. I could tell something was on his mind.

Then I discovered a fascinating parallel between the life of Job and the life of Reverend Alan. As I helped him wheel three carts out to his car, he told me about an extremely difficult situation that he's been facing.

It seems that someone is harassing Reverend Alan. It started out innocently enough. This person initially came to the pastor for a few counseling sessions. But these weekly one-hour sessions evolved into daily meetings in which this poor lost soul would go off on tangents that began to frighten Reverend Alan. It became clear that this guy was delusional. He thought he had a direct line to God and knew all the answers. He would lecture Reverend Alan at length about "spiritual matters" and chide the pastor for his "iniquities."

It got to be too much. Reverend Alan gently suggested that since the two of them didn't agree theologically, maybe the man should seek a different church. But the man didn't take the hint. He told Reverend Alan that he admired him more than any person on earth. He wouldn't dream of leaving. Reverend Alan tried another tactic. He told the guy he was cured and there was no need for further counseling. After a respite of a few days, the nut began to show up at the pastor's home, often late at night, and go on at length about some obscure theological point. Apparently this nut has even broken into the pastor's home. Although the man never threatened violence, the pastor was afraid.

As he started his car, I told Reverend Alan that I thought I could help him because I've been studying the book of Job. When he was at his lowest, four friends came to visit Job. They each offered their opinion about why Job was facing these trials and what they meant. Fortunately, I've memorized most of the book of Job, so I recited the relevant chapters to Reverend Alan as he rolled up his car window.

As he slowly backed out of his parking space, I assured the pastor that he wasn't suffering because of his own sin. God doesn't work that way. Jogging slowly alongside his car, I shouted through the rolled-up window that we don't know why we suffer, but that we should simply fear the Lord and trust his judgment. As Reverend Alan sped off I yelled after him, "A wise man submits to the will of God and does not question divine justice!"

Ultimately, Job remains utterly faithful to God through all of this adversity and proves Satan wrong. I'm sure Reverend Alan will survive this current trial, too, and be the better for it. God is always just, although we cannot always see it from our limited perspective. Ultimately, God rewarded Job with more wealth and happiness than he'd had before. I trust the same will happen to my pastor. At the moment he's just not himself, but I don't think he realizes it. Some people just lack self-awareness.

Chapter Six

The Sound of Music

Psalms, Proverbs, Ecclesiastes, Song of Solomon

AUSTIN

F irst off, I'd like to apologize.

If this chapter seems more confused than usual, it's because I've been feeling really terrible lately. I don't know what it is. It's like the worst cold I've ever had. It came up all of a sudden, and I blame those rotten kids at my son's preschool—those two-year-olds who pick their noses with such fierce dedication and can't be bothered to wipe them. They've obviously never heard of Kleenex. At that age they probably haven't heard of much, but still—they run around all day with these horribly thick, runny yellow mustaches, and it's pretty gross. Last week, I knelt down to tie the shoe of one of these disease merchants, and when he sneezed at point-blank range, I got a face full of toddler snot.

Ever since, I've just been so out of it. I'm sneezing up a storm and have wiped my nose so red and raw it feels like it's going to fall off.

I knew we had a deadline coming up so I called Reed to see if he would be willing to take over the task of writing chapter 6. In that beautiful Christian way I've always loved about him, he said, "This is what you get, you stupid atheist. God is punishing you for your pagan ways. You're going straight to hell. Besides, I'm way behind on chapter 9."

I called my publisher and asked if I might have some extra time to recover. We had a lovely conversation on a variety of topics, but ultimately the phrases "hefty advance" and "we'll sue your lazy butt" made me understand that I had better get back to work.

Meanwhile, I continued to shudder under my covers, feeling absolutely miserable and wanting my mommy. I knew I wouldn't be able to speak with her, though, and cursed the day I shut her in that rest home with no windows and no phone.

In my weakened and lonely state, I desperately wanted succor, but then I looked up the word and discovered it didn't mean what I thought it did.

So with nowhere else to turn, I went back to work researching the Bible.

And lo and behold, I found what I needed.

As it happened, I had reached what I call the musical interlude of the Bible, the books of songs and poetry called Psalms, Proverbs, Ecclesiastes, and Song of Solomon. This is arguably the most reflective section of the Bible, reflective in the sense that it's a thoughtful consideration of God and life and being human, but also in the sense that you can see yourself in it.

Contrary to what you might think, however, the famous Twenty-third Psalm offered me absolutely no comfort. "The Lord is my shepherd"?! Surely this is somebody's idea of a sick joke. Is a shepherd really the most caring and protective metaphor we can think of? Shepherds take care of sheep, all right: under their care, sheep are sheared, castrated, and led to slaughter. And as has already been mentioned, in some parts of the world shepherds perform certain acts with sheep that can only be described as intrusive. I'll take care of myself, thank you very much. No wonder mutton tastes terrible.

I think the people who recite the Twenty-third Psalm as a prayer or mantra have never actually read it. Or haven't really listened to it. Or something. Maybe it's me, but I don't find the following words all that reassuring:

The Lord is my Shepherd; I shall not want.

He maketh me to lie down and think of England.

He restoreth my soul: he leadeth me into trucks and slaughterhouses for his dinner's sake.

Yea, though I walk through the valley of the shadow of death, I will fear no wolf. At least with a wolf you get a fair shot at sniffing him out before he gets too close and maybe making a run for it.

But thou art with me; thy rod and thy staff comfort me, for they are nowhere near as terrible as thy knife, which cutteth my testicles off.

Thou preparest a table with me in the presence of mine enemies: thou anointest my head with oil and garlic butter; my cup runneth over with a nice cabernet, a little mint sauce, and some lovely roast potatoes.

Surely goodness and mercy shall follow me all the days of my life (without ever catching up), and I will dwell in the house of the Lord forever, where the rent is cheap and the roof leaks. (New Revised Contemporary Translation)

Needless to say, I turned to other Psalms for comfort. Fortunately, Psalms is like a collection of K-Tel's greatest hits—there are songs for every topic. I wanted something that would assure me things would be all right. I turned to Psalm 8, which describes the majesty and wonder of God's creation. Unfortunately, lines such as, "You made the earth and the heavens and I am like an ant under thy mighty Birkenstocks," don't make my manly bosom swell with feelings of self-worth. In fact, my confusion is perfectly expressed in Psalm 42:

> I don't understand You
> I don't get You at all
> You make me feel at sixes and sevens
> My brain is akimbo, everything's bassackwards
> I'm all shook up.[12]

---

[12]"Psalm 42," you'll remember, was one of Elvis Presley's biggest hits.

So I stuck with the party psalms, the ones that urge us to make a joyful noise unto the Lord. In fact, the Bible beat Elton John and the Bay City Rollers by several millennia with the very first "Saturday Night" song (Psalm 66):

> It's Saturday night
> Everything's all right
> Another week's gone by
> And no one's slaughtered our people already
> So come out of the temple
> Get up off the floor
> The Sabbath is over
> Let's pray some more.
> (Chorus)
> Saturday, Saturday
> This is the night to enjoy
> Saturday, gotta say
> Oy oy oy!

My favorites, though, have to be Psalms 120–134, the songs for pilgrims traveling to Jerusalem.

> From the north, south
> East and west
> We're going to the city
> We know is the best
> We're gonna get high high high
> In Jerusalem
> We'll be flying high high high
> In Jerusalem
> We'll be so high
> It won't be odd
> We'll touch the sky
> And the face of God
> In Jerusalem
> If we think we can
> Then we know we will
> Reach Jerusalem
> The city on the hill

And we'll be so high high high
In Jerusalem
The air is thin and dry dry dry
In Jerusalem
We'll say our prayers
We'll be devout
If we get some air
And don't pass out
In Jerusalem.

Reading that, I began to feel a slight tingling sensation, as if I was coming into the presence of the Almighty or had accidentally overmedicated myself. Was God preparing to make Himself known to me? Was I coming close to my own Jerusalem? Was my confused agnostic soul about to meet its theological Waterloo?

No. I was dehydrated. I chugged a gallon of water and moved on to Proverbs.

In my fever-addled wooziness, the list of aphorisms and life lessons that make up Proverbs served as an excellent pre-flight checklist. I resolved never to cosign a loan (Proverbs 6:1–5). I promised myself to always treat others honestly (Proverbs 11:1–3). I vowed to teach my children well (Crosby, Stills, Nash & Young). I agreed that it is better to dwell in a corner of the housetop than with a brawling woman in a wide house, even though I had no idea what that meant (Proverbs 9). I couldn't argue that a bird in the hand is worth two in the bush (*Poor Richard's Almanack*), and even though I wanted to quibble about the size of the bird and the kind of bush, I didn't.

But really, this kind of deathbed self-analysis was beginning to feel funereal, a feeling not helped by the book of Ecclesiastes, the entire contents of which can be summed up in one line: "Oh Lord, what the hell is the point?"

I'm sorry, but this book is a bummer. From the very first line—"Nothing makes sense"—Ecclesiastes (from the Greek word meaning "John Cleese's testes") revels in a kind of morose cynicism that I'm all too familiar with at the best of times and am positively drowning in here on my bed of pain. The litany of complaints goes on and on: nothing ever changes, everything's happened before, life is short, and money can't buy me love. Well, that's just terrific. On top of all that good news, we still have to respect and obey God. Hardly seems worth it.

But then I turned to the Song of Solomon and suddenly it was as if I'd wandered into the *Penthouse Forum*. This is a love song, baby: a passionate, uninhibited erotic poem. I couldn't believe it. I was struck by lines such as:

> His fruit was sweet to my taste. . . .
> Thy lips are like honey. . . .
> Thy neck is like the Tower of David. . . .
> Thy breasts are like two deer. . . .
> Thy temples are like a pomegranate. . . .

I don't know about you, but any mention of pomegranates gets me hot.

> Thy teeth are like Tic-Tacs, sweet and minty. . . .
> Thy hair is like a flock of goats, leaving little chocolate candies on the side of a hill. . . .
> Thy spleen is red and rare, like a ruby, but not as funny as thy pancreas, which hath the all-important K sound. . . .
> Thy small intestine is long and curvy, like the road to Jerusalem, but with fewer soldiers carrying AK-47s. . . .

And so on.

Woof.

This left me in quite a state, as you can imagine. I was too weak to get out of bed, but with the words of Solomon's love song echoing in my brain, I began to . . . it's difficult to describe . . . I reached down and started to . . . how do I say this . . . well, in the spirit of my great biblical hero Onan, I . . . no reason to be shy about, I guess . . . I began to . . . to pleasure myself.

But not for long.

Remember how I mentioned my nose was so red and raw it felt as if it would fall off? Well, that's not what fell off first.

You're way ahead of me here, aren't you?

Exactly. *That* fell off first.

Apparently, I had more than a cold.

Chapter Seven

The Books Nobody Has Ever Really Read

What Actually Happens in Obadiah, Micah, Habakkuk, Nahum, and Haggai?

REED

Okay, by a show of hands, has anyone who is reading this book actually read the Bible cover to cover? Come on. Tell the truth. It isn't surprising that Average Joe Citizen hasn't read the Good Book all the way through, but it is shocking that even people who claim to be Bible experts have often not read the whole thing. How can one be critical about the Bible without having experienced it in its entirety? It would be like a movie critic reviewing a movie after only seeing the trailer.

I conducted extensive national polling and have found that the five least-read books of the Bible are Obadiah, Micah, Habakkuk, Nahum, and Haggai. *Ulysses* by James Joyce was the sixth least-read book, but there is some question about whether or not it is actually part of the Old Testament. Obadiah, Micah, Habakkuk, Nahum, and Haggai are five of the twelve so-called Minor Prophets, along with Hosea, Joel, Amos, Jonah, Zephaniah, Zechariah, and Malachi. But Obadiah, Micah, Habakkuk, Nahum, and Haggai are the most obscure of the Minor Prophets. They are, if you will, the "Minor Minor Prophets."

The Minor Prophets were all under the age of consent— hence the name. This, however, is misleading because in Bible times the age of consent was much older than it is today. Life spans were longer back then. Most folks lived to be several hundred years old and the age of consent reflected this. You were considered a full adult not at age twenty-one, but at age seventy-five. Although it was not legal to buy alcohol until age seventy-five, you could join the army or get married without parental consent at age seventy-two. Once you hit your sixty-fifth birthday you were allowed to buy cigarettes, although all the kids knew which shop owners would sell tobacco to the underaged sixty-two-year-olds.

These long life spans caused all kinds of social problems. There were no retirement homes in those days, so all the generations of a family lived under a single roof. This was not easy. For instance, Methuselah lived to be 969 years old. At the age of seventy-eight, Methuselah retired and moved in with the family of his oldest daughter, who was thirty-eight at the time. He stayed with that family for the next 881 years. Methuselah was active and sharp well into his late 600s, but then began to slow down and became something of a burden on his daughter for the next three hundred years. She was glad to look after her father, but she didn't have the energy she'd had before falling and breaking her hip at age 587.

As each succeeding generation reached its late seventies, they retired and moved in with their children. At the time of Methuselah's death there were thirty generations, a total of 637 people, living in the one house with a single toilet and almost no closet space. This is why so many wise men left home and wandered in the desert. These men were wise not so much for seeking God as for getting away from the hundreds of nieces and nephews and great-great-great-grandkids arguing over which one got to take a bath this month.

But I digress. The point is that the Minor Prophets were not actually all that young.

Incidentally, if you find this section of the book instructive, please drop a note to the publisher. I'm hoping this chapter will fulfill part of the community service I'm required to do for violating the restraining order mistakenly taken out on me in the name of my pastor. Anyway, in what I hope is a public service, what follows is a brief overview—Cliff Notes, if you will—of each of the five least-read books, the *really* minor books of the Old Testament. Let me say that these overviews are in no way a substitute for the actual experience of reading these books in their entirety, and I hope someday to read them all the way through myself.

Obadiah

The name *Obadiah* means "worshiper of the Lord." It is the shortest book in the Old Testament, consisting of only one chapter. Obadiah was written shortly after the Babylonians and Edomites (who are more well-known for their cheese-making prowess) conquered Judah in 586 B.C.

There are two famous quotes from Obadiah. The first is, "As you have done, so it will be done to you." And boy, oh boy, did the Babylonians do it to the people of Judah. The second famous quote from Obadiah is, "I knew John Kennedy. You're no John Kennedy."

Obadiah delivers the main message of the Old Testament in a single chapter. He condemns the people for their sinfulness, but predicts that ultimately God will prevail and all nations will follow God.

Other Old Testament prophets deliver a similar message in a much more long-winded way, but I admire Obadiah for his succinctness. He doesn't waste our time. He is short and to the point. He gets right to it. He doesn't repeat the same thing in different words over and over. This is a writing style to which I aspire. I'd like to write like Obadiah. I don't want to repeat myself. I just want to say things once. I don't want to be repetitive.

Obadiah was ahead of his time. He foresaw shorter attention spans. In verses 17–23 Obadiah predicts the development of fast food and *Reader's Digest*.

Micah

Micah takes six chapters to deliver the same message that Obadiah delivers in a single chapter. Micah consists of a series of six prophecies that are written as poems. In order, the six poems predict doom, then salvation, doom, then salvation, doom, then . . . wait for it . . . salvation.

That humankind is sinful but the Messiah is on the way is the message of almost all the Old Testament prophets. It isn't completely clear why people needed to hear the same message in umpteen different ways, but it could have to do with the "Methuselah Factor" (see above). An extremely old population would have had bad eyesight and hearing, so the message of salvation may not have been understood the first eighty-three times it was delivered. In any case, as Austin pointed out so eloquently in chapter 4, the Old Testament proves that endless sequels to popular stories are not a new phenomenon.

Though often attributed to Andy Warhol, it was actually Micah who floated the notion that in the future everyone would be famous for fifteen minutes. Andy Warhol took it and ran with it. Micah's influence on Andy Warhol is also evident in Warhol's multiple images of Marilyn Monroe and Campbell's soup cans. Warhol repeated images in the same way that Micah repeated the message of doom followed by salvation three times. But the most striking similarity between Micah and Andy Warhol was that they each had only a single idea that they repeated again and again.

Nahum

Like the names of so many prophets, the name *Nahum* has significance. Nahum had postnasal drip, so he cleared his throat a lot. And if you say the name Nahum aloud, you will immediately observe that it is strikingly similar to the sound one makes when clearing one's throat.

It is also significant that Nahum means "comfort" and that he prophesied in the southern kingdom of Judah. Southern Comfort apparently played a large role in Nahum's life. There is strong archeological evidence that he drank a bit. He was an embarrassment to the other prophets. Every time the prophets got together, Nahum would drink and make a scene. One time he made a pass at a camel. But his most infamous drunken prank was when he waited for just the right moment and then pointed off in the distance and screamed, "Look! It's the Messiah! He's arrived! The Messiah is finally here!" As all the other prophets scrambled to see the newly arrived Messiah, Nahum said, "Made you look! Made you look!" It is for this reason Nahum is not mentioned in any other book of the Bible. The other prophets wanted to pretend he didn't exist.

We find further evidence that Nahum was generally pickled in the very first verse of the book. Nahum begins, "I am Nahum from Elkosh." The trouble is that there is no village named Elkosh. There never was. Nahum was so sauced that he slurred the name of his hometown as he dictated this book to his scribe.

Like two other minor prophets, Jonah and Micah, Nahum focuses on the eventual destruction of Assyria in retribution for its mistreatment of Judah and Israel. The book opens with an alphabetic psalm, or acrostic. Reverend Alan says that the text of Nahum must have been altered because verses 9–11 of chapter 1 don't fit with the rhyming scheme. He is wrong. These verses were not added later. Nahum was just so plastered that he lost track of the poetic scheme.

The terror that Nahum predicted would befall the Assyrians did come to pass. Nineveh was thoroughly destroyed and its ruins were not uncovered again until 1845. Apparently it was actually Nahum who single-handedly destroyed the town, on a wild camel ride through Nineveh after a bender at the local tavern.

Habakkuk

The book of Habakkuk records a conversation between the prophet Habakkuk and God, so in some sense it is similar to the popular Bill Cosby routine that depicts a conversation between Noah and God. The prophet wonders why God isn't punishing the sinful people of Judah. God answers that they will be punished by the Babylonians. Habakkuk thinks it's unfair to have the Babylonians punish the Jews. He thinks the Jews are better than the Babylonians, who deserve punishment themselves. God tells him to stop being such a tattletale. He gives Habakkuk that old line about how two wrongs don't make a right. God says he'll deal with the Babylonians later, but for now He'll have them punish the Jews. Habakkuk asks God who will win the Super Bowl because he wants to place a bet. God says he can't tell him. Habakkuk questions God's omnipotence. God questions Habakkuk's potency.

According to one of the Bible's strangest legends, an angel transported Habakkuk from Judah to Babylon to deliver a bowl of stew to Daniel in the lions' den. Yep. Stew. And then the angel took Habakkuk back home, leaving Daniel still in the lions' den. The legend doesn't mention Daniel's reaction, but I'm guessing that as they were leaving Daniel behind he said something like, "Hey! Where are you going? Let me out! I'm still in here with the lions, remember? And I don't even like stew!" But, as I say, that's just a guess.

It is said that one verse from this obscure book launched the Protestant Reformation. Habakkuk 2:4 says, "The just shall live by faith." Martin Luther seized on this idea, as paraphrased in Romans 1:17. His point was that salvation is the result of faith in God, and not of church rituals. The pope told Martin Luther that this was blasphemy and sent him to Minnesota, where millions of Lutherans still reside today.

Habakkuk laments the evil he sees all around him. He asks God to send the Deliverer now. God tells him to wait patiently for the Messiah, that all will unfold in God's time. It's like if you order a pizza when you are really hungry. You know it will eventually arrive, but it's still hard to wait. Worrying about the pizza will not make it come faster. It will be delivered in thirty minutes or less and, if not, it will be free. That is God's lesson in Habakkuk.

Haggai

The book of Haggai was written in 520 B.C. We know the precise date because Haggai made a note of it when he wrote the book. He said that he wrote the book the second year that Darius was king of Persia. We know from historical records that that year was 520 B.C. The copyright office has also confirmed this date.

The name *Haggai* means "festival." This probably means that Haggai was born on one of the Jewish holidays, most likely either Passover or Labor Day. Haggai was well over seventy years old when he wrote the book because he mentions that he remembers the glorious temple of Solomon that had been destroyed sixty-six years earlier. Haggai also mentions that he was best friends with Adam and Eve, so rather than being elderly, Haggai may have simply been delusional.

Haggai admonishes the Jews for not yet having rebuilt the temple in Jerusalem although it has been nearly twenty years since they returned from their exile in Babylon. He asks them, "Is it right for you to live in expensive houses, while my temple is a pile of ruins?" The people know they have been negligent and get right to work trying to locate a mortgage broker.

There are at least of couple of reasons the Jews had abandoned work on rebuilding the temple. First, the Persian king who had ruled over Jerusalem up until only a year before this prophecy had forbidden them from rebuilding the temple. Second, they needed to save ten percent for a down payment. And if they wanted to avoid paying mortgage insurance and get a decent interest rate, they needed to put twenty percent down. It was a daunting prospect that is still common for first-time temple owners.

Reverend Alan and I had a discussion recently on this very topic while I was visiting him in the television lounge of the group home where he is now recuperating. I suggested we turn the channel from *Mister Rogers' Neighborhood* to CNBC to check on interest rates. He began to pant and shake uncontrollably. He insisted he wanted to watch *Mister Rogers*. I pushed the point. Maybe God wants us to keep track of the economy. Perhaps God determined at the beginning of time that at this moment in history we were not supposed to be watching *Mister Rogers*. Should we contradict God? At this point the pastor fell to the floor crying. I got a little nostalgic because my little sister used to react the same way when I'd use this line of reasoning to get her to watch a ballgame instead of *The Smurfs*. The orderlies came over and restrained Reverend Alan. As he was being taken to his room he called, "This is what God wants, isn't it? Are you happy now? This must be God's will!" And my answer was "Yes," I was happy. My pastor finally agreed with me about predestination. I feel closer to him than ever before.

But back to Haggai. What was it that motivated the people of Israel to get to work on the temple? Guilt? Faith? Nope, it was bribery. They had just suffered through a bad harvest and the economy was not doing very well, so Haggai promises that God will richly bless them if they rebuild the temple. The lesson we learn is, "Do God's work and you will be rewarded with earthly riches." This is a lesson that is still valuable today, especially to televangelists.

The governor of Judah was named Zerubbabel. I'm not making this name up. Zerubbabel organized the rebuilding work, so Haggai prophesies that Zerubbabel will become the long-awaited Messiah. But no matter how much Zerubbabel begs, Haggai won't agree to name the temple after him for fear that everyone would think the name was a joke. Furious, Zerubbabel changes his name to Chip and leaves town.

That Haggai's prophecy about Zerubbabel did not come true brings up a very interesting point. Back when he was still capable of putting together whole sentences, Reverend Alan told me that prophecy always comes true either in the short term or in the long term. I say that sometimes prophecy is just wrong and people justify it by saying we haven't yet given it enough time.

I'd like to share with you a lesson about prophecy that I learned as a fourth grader in Vacation Bible School at the Grace Reformed Church. Although I come from a family of devout Presbyterians, my parents approved of any church that preached the word of God. On the first day of VBS at this pagan church, we were all given a little kitten to take home. We were to care for it and watch it grow, just as God cares for us and helps us grow. On the final day of VBS two weeks later, I commented to the pastor that my little kitten hadn't grown. He said, "It will, Reed. You just wait." So I went home and saw that the kitten was asleep. I watched it every day. It never moved. A few weeks later it started to smell and my dad buried it. It never did get any bigger. The pastor was wrong. (For the sake of clarity, I want to state for the record that this was *not* Reverend Alan. He would be incapable of such a travesty. For one thing, he's allergic to cats.) I don't know, maybe I should have fed the kitten. Anyway, that pagan pastor's prediction was just like Haggai's— wrong, wrong, wrong.

The book of Haggai ends before the temple is completed. The most likely explanation is that Haggai died before the temple was finished, probably in a tragic construction accident. Don't forget, these were the days before OSHA existed and even today it's not the best idea for a man in his midseventies (and possibly senile) to be working on a construction site. But I blame Haggai for his own death. He was a prophet. He should have seen it coming.

To fully understand the meaning of the book of Haggai and to properly interpret it, we must also closely study the book that follows it, Zechariah, as well as the books of Malachi and Daniel. But we won't.

Chapter Eight

Apocrypha Now

The Books They
Don't Want You to See

AUSTIN

Leprosy. Ever hear of it?
People don't catch it much anymore, maybe 150 cases a year in the United States. Unfortunately, I fall into that five percent of people who aren't immune to the bacillus *Mycobacterium leprae*. I couldn't catch the relatively benign tuberculosis, oh no. That's a disease great writers get. No, I had to get what my doctor calls, trying to sound upbeat but really blowing smoke up my skirt, "a minor case of leprosy." Which is like being a little bit pregnant or catching a minor case of death.

Jesus healed the lepers, you know. But that was then and this is now. For one thing, we tend not to see too many living deities these days. People talk about a Second Coming, but I think that maybe they're being optimistic. I think God probably saw how little effect His Son's death had the last time, reread Ecclesiastes with its Eeyore-like gloominess and said, "Man, you got that right. Couldn't have said it better Myself."

I keep clinging to the hope that this is just a really bad cold, but it's hard to ignore the truth when your manhood drops off in your hand. Come to think of it, my hands themselves have also started looking a little shriveled and nubby.

71

This book is definitely going to suffer from *missed deadlinitus* if I lose too many fingers.

They never tell you what you need to know. You know? Nobody ever told me I had to watch out for *leprosy*, for God's sake. That's like lying awake nights worrying about the plague or being pecked to death by a dodo. You never think it's going to happen to you. When I think of all that money I wasted on prostate exams. Ten or twelve prostate exams a year now seem like such a frivolous indulgence. They felt great, *but at what cost?*

I admit it, with my mortality staring me smack in the face, I went through an intensive self-examination. (Not a physical one, and not because I'm worried about discovering lumps. Cancer seems like such a nonissue now. I'm just afraid of discovering more missing appendages.) No, I mean a spiritual self-examination. I'm suddenly regretting the roads not taken, the words left unsaid, the deeds left undone. I made a list of all the things I never accomplished:

- I never learned to play the guitar.

- I never told my family I love them.

- I never slept with a supermodel.

- Never told a supermodel I love her.

- Never spoke to a supermodel.

- Wouldn't know what to do with a supermodel if she bit me on the behind.

- Never had a supermodel bite me on the behind.

The list goes on.

I got angry. (I've been through denial. I spent all of chapter 6 telling myself this was a bad case of the *sniffles*.) I raged.

I screamed at the heavens. I cursed the Lord, demanding to know *why me?* Then I thought of the irony of a latent atheist screaming at the Lord and cursed myself for being such a hypocrite. Then I remembered that, just like in foxholes and airplanes with turbulence, there are no atheists in a one-man leper colony, so I got off my own back. Before it broke off.

I raged at my ignorance and started searching for clues. I kept feeling that I should have known. I should have seen it coming. And then I happened upon the Apocrypha, the hidden books of the Bible. And I thought "ah-ha!" I'd found my smoking gun.

The Apocrypha is a collection of stories and lessons that through a vast worldwide conspiracy were systematically left out of the Bible. One glance at this fiery material told me this was no mere clerical error. Corrupt governments and sinister "shadow churches" deliberately covered up this stuff in order to deceive a credulous world.[13] These are the same people who cover up the truth about extraterrestrial life, the JFK assassination, and the popularity of John Tesh.

Some of the Apocrypha is harmless first-draft stuff that was obviously never intended for publication—like these early rejected Proverbs:

> "A man is only as old as the woman he feels."
> "Never put off until tomorrow that which you can put
>   off until the day after tomorrow."

Some of it is gross, like the story of Tobit, who goes against Assyrian law and gives proper burial to executed Jews. For this "crime," he's blinded by sparrow droppings that fall into his eyes, and his eyesight is only restored when the archangel Raphael instructs that his eyes be smeared with the bile of a fish. Archangel Raphael was obviously a better painter than he was a doctor.

Some of it is sexist. The stories of Judith and Susanna illustrate the inherently evil nature of women who refuse to

---

[13]Like that? Oliver Stone helped me write it.

sleep with respected Jewish leaders. Judith even goes so far as to cut off a general's head, and then, just for giggles, she cuts off the general's privates. Yes, it's sexist and hateful, but charmingly so.

And some of it is just bizarre. The Prayer of Azariah and the Song of the Three Jews was deleted from the book of Daniel, probably because it describes in such weird detail how Abednego, Shadrach, and Meshach survived in the fiery furnace. Apparently, while the flames leapt up around them and they suffered the torments of hell, they survived by singing:

> Oh it was sad, so sad
> It was sad, so sad
> It was sad when that great ship went down
> To the bottom of the—
> Uncles and aunts, little children lost their pants
> It was sad when that great ship went down.

You see? Bizarre.

But the real apocryphal meat comes in Macadamias 1–4, the so-called Book of Nuts. This is where the rubber hits the road, where the important distinctions between that which is spiritual and that which is merely religious are spelled out. Reading these, you can clearly understand why certain people would want these books covered up. Macadamias reveals the "how-to" of religious worship is not as it has always appeared.

First Macadamia says quite clearly:

> Do not thou give thy hard-earned cash to televangelists, who prey on thy weakness and gullibility, and have terrible hair to boot.

This lesson is implied throughout the Bible (when Jesus rousts the moneylenders) and by Pink Floyd (when they sing "Money / Is a crime . . .") but nowhere is it stated so specifically as it is here.

Second Macadamia goes on to say:

> Thou shalt not try to convert a man who already hath a
> perfectly good faith in his own religion. Nor shalt thou
> kill this other merely because his beliefs and customs
> are strange to you.

It's clear that "shadow churches" are working in tandem with arms manufacturers to keep this one under wraps. Think of all the ammunition that's been sold and fired in the name of one god or another. More importantly, think of the people who've rung your doorbell during dinner, interrupting a private family meal or a really important televised sporting event, to pester you about how their religion is so much better than yours, and how their God can kick your God's butt, and how if you'd just read their pamphlet, it'd make your life much better in so many ways, like it's some ridiculous theological chain-letter. And have you ever noticed that all these people who want you to listen to what they have to say never want to hear what *you* have to say? Second Macadamia would make them go away.

I should make it clear that when I use the phrase "shadow church," I'm not referring to any of the world's established churches, which, to a congregation, are extremely tolerant of other viewpoints and alternative lifestyles. No, I'm speaking of specific rogue elements, sinister operatives working behind the scenes to pull the strings and make established church leaders jump and do their bidding like some twisted Howdy Doody. These miscreants have their hands up the robes of established clerics, making them jerk and jitter like a depraved Miss Piggy. (I mean an even more depraved Miss Piggy.) Choose your forced metaphor. The point is, we're being made to dance and we don't even get to choose the DJ.

Third Macadamia reveals that devotion to God isn't dependent on a building. Developing the idea that God is everywhere, it tries to undermine the powerful influence of religious architecture. It reveals that the word *church* comes from the Greek word meaning, "sound you make while puking," and the word *synagogue* comes from the Hebrew for "I'm agog at all the sin in here." Similarly, Third Macadamia points out that a *temple* is something Abraham Lincoln was shot in. You can see how dangerous it'd be if this got out.

Finally, 4 Macadamia posits a series of Solomon-like logical arguments:

> Whereas, the right to worship freely is clearly understood; and
>
> Whereas, the government should stay out of all matters pertaining to religion; then
>
> Therefore, the church should stay the hell out of politics. Or be taxed.

This is self-evident, and might once have been biblical law. But because of its relegation to the disputed books of the Apocrypha, arguments about school prayer and the Ten Commandments and whose god gets to be mentioned on the money continue to this day. On the other hand, taxpayer dollars weren't spent on the creation of *Joseph and the Amazing Technicolor Dreamcoat*, so maybe things are working out just fine.

You can see I've moved through Anger and Bargaining and finally reached Acceptance. There are several reasons for this. The first is that my normal predisposition toward the Ecclesiastes-like cynicism of "What's the point?" has been replaced by a more fatalistic *laissez-faire* attitude of "Whatcha gonna do?" And really, what *am* I gonna do? Short of a miracle, which I don't believe in, you don't recover from leprosy.

But the freedom of that acceptance gave me an almost scientific detachment, and allowed me to watch the deterioration—the physical detachment, if you will—of my body with some amusement. Because really, when you think about it, it's pretty funny. My fingers started swelling up and finally dropped off, one by one, like overripe persimmons going *splat* on the bricks. I ended up typing these last two pages using my left elbow and my nose, until I typed an emphatic period three paragraphs ago and left two nostrils and lots of cartilage sitting on my keyboard. I'm finishing up typing this paragraph using only my remaining eight toes. The good news is that I'm now finally limber enough to take up Buddhism.

And then, finally, the inevitable happened. Two days ago, at 3:33 in the afternoon, I died. I was pronounced dead at Cedars-Sinai Hospital and buried six feet underground in a beautiful grave in Forest Lawn Cemetery, overlooking the Walt Disney Studios and beautiful downtown Burbank.

And then things got *really* interesting.

Chapter Nine

The Gospels

Religion and Politics

REED

First, let me say that this chapter is dedicated to Austin. I was going to dedicate the entire book to him, but at this point I don't know if it will ever be completed. Austin died leaving two chapters unwritten. I still have two chapters of my own to finish and I don't necessarily have the time or inclination to do Austin's work too. I'm not saying I'm mad at him for dying before finishing the book, but I will say that it is very inconvenient for me.

I am shocked and saddened by Austin's passing. I knew him well. We collaborated on six plays, three books, four radio series and a television pilot that never got picked up. I pray for his family and know their finances will be fine if they prevail in their current litigation with me over Austin's portion of our royalties.

We never know when our time will be up. Leprosy—who would have thought? I know that Austin was beginning to look for spiritual answers near the end of his life. I don't know whether he had found God by the time he died. But it is not for us to judge. That is up to God. I will leave it in His hands.

So while Austin burns in hell, let's talk about Jesus.

Let me preface this discussion by saying that I am a Democrat, actually the only Democrat in my entire family. I come from a long line of Republicans. My parents are Republicans. My three siblings are Republicans. All of my grandparents were Republicans. The name *Franklin Delano Roosevelt* caused my grandparents to grumble and throw their eyes to heaven in the same way I do when I hear the name *Ronald Reagan.* You see, for them FDR was the beginning of the end of small government. He bloated the federal government. He created a vast bureaucracy in Washington. He took away states' rights. He gave both of my Republican grandfathers jobs in the CCC and WPA during the Depression. Okay, although the last sentence was true, they usually left that part out. Anyway, you get the gist of the way the rest of my family feels about Democrats.

So imagine my surprise when I read the Gospels and discovered that Jesus was a Republican.

To be honest, I never thought of Jesus as either a Republican or a Democrat. I'd always been inclined to believe that Jesus didn't have a political affiliation. Well, what I found in my research has shaken me to my Democratic/Presbyterian core.

The first indication that Jesus was likely a Republican is that he was born poor. Many of the leading Republican figures such as Abraham Lincoln and Richard Nixon were born poor or in the lower middle class and through hard work pulled themselves up by their bootstraps. This life experience led them to believe in the conservative ideology— that anyone can better himself or herself if they just work at it. Conversely, many Democratic politicians were born wealthy—folks like Franklin Roosevelt and John Kennedy. Through an accident of birth they were blessed with many worldly possessions and they spent their adult lives working to see that the less fortunate were taken care of by the government. So by his poor status at birth Jesus would have been conservatively inclined.

Actually, Jesus' life was remarkably similar to the lives of many of our Republican presidents. Like Ronald Reagan, Jesus was a great communicator. Like Lincoln, Jesus was killed at his greatest moment of triumph. Like Nixon, Jesus was unfairly persecuted. Like Eisenhower, Jesus was prematurely bald.

Now you may be thinking, "But Jesus looked after the less fortunate, so he must have been a Democrat." This thinking is half-correct, but also paints Republicans in an unfairly negative way. It isn't only the Democrats who want the poor to be better off. Republicans would like the poor to do better, but through hard work and not government handouts. And while Jesus did look after the poor and instructed his followers to do the same, he didn't suggest that anyone help the poor through government programs. His work with the poor was all done privately. This is the conservative way. He told the rich man to sell all he had, give it to the poor and follow him. Jesus fed the five thousand not with food stamps, but with his own miracle. Jesus healed the sick privately, not in public hospitals funded with your tax dollars.

And on the subject of public assistance, it is worth noting that although Jesus' disciples gave up their jobs to follow him, there is no indication that any of them collected unemployment benefits or welfare. It simply was not Jesus' way to let government do work that private individuals should be doing. For goodness sake, Jesus didn't even allow himself a public defender at the time of his trial.

Like a good Republican, Jesus also worked to reduce bureaucracy. Before he came along, the Jewish religious laws were burdensome and complicated. Jesus simplified these laws. He told the people to ignore old laws and he gave them a new, simpler code to live by that involved only two rules. First, love the Lord thy God with all thy heart and all thy soul and all thy mind. Second, love thy neighbor as thyself. It was straightforward. It was simple. It was conservative.

The life of Jesus also teaches us a lesson about the dangers of government overreaching its boundaries. Don't forget that it was the government, in the person of Pontius Pilate, that brought about Jesus' death. In a similar way, the CIA brought about the deaths of Vince Foster, John Kennedy, and the end of Burt Reynolds's career. Why can't the government just leave people alone?

Along these lines, I've been having trouble tracking down Reverend Alan since he left the group home several weeks ago. I think the CIA might be behind it. You see, his former church says they have no forwarding address for him. Plus, Reverend Alan's old phone number is no longer in service. I was worried about Reverend Alan, so I hired a private investigator to track him down. The good news is that he is okay and living with his parents. Apparently they are very private people. They have an unlisted phone number. And a large new gate around their home. And an expensive security system. Anyway, I camped outside their compound for several days waiting for the pastor. He came out once and I thought he saw me, but he rushed back into the house. After a week or so I ran out of food and left the premises to go shopping. When I got back the house was abandoned. It sure looks like the work of the CIA to me.

I could go on and on with further examples of Jesus' conservatism, but by now you get the point. Undoubtedly, Jesus was a member of the GOP. This is not to say, however, that there is no contradictory evidence to Jesus' conservatism. There are indications that Jesus may have been more liberal in his younger days. Remember, with the exception of one incident when Jesus was twelve years old, the Bible tells us nothing about him between his birth and the beginning of his ministry at age thirty. Like so many of us, he likely had more liberal views during his college years. We can see occasional vestiges of his old liberalism in certain behaviors later on. Perhaps these mean that Jesus was a middle-of-the-road Republican rather than a staunch right-winger.

First of all, Jesus liked to associate with the lower classes and not wealthy establishment types. This is very un-Republican. Jesus shocked the establishment by spending much of his time with prostitutes and tax collectors. This is more likely to be the behavior of a Democrat (or a televangelist) than a Republican. Republicans don't spend time with prostitutes because they don't have sex. And Democrats love to tax and spend, so they enjoy the company of tax collectors.

Like another moderate Republican, President George Bush, Jesus showed weakness on the tax issue. President Bush alienated the far right when he said, "Read my lips, no new taxes," and then changed his mind. Jesus told people to "Render unto Caesar what is Caesar's"—namely, taxes and salad.

But these are small points. The overall picture of Jesus as a political conservative is undeniable. Ultimately, two pieces of evidence convinced me of this. The first was the way that Jesus reacted in the desert when tempted by Satan. Did he yield to temptation? Absolutely not. He "just said no." Thank you, Nancy Reagan. Second, and most convincingly, Jesus' mission was to dictate to others how they should behave in their private lives and to inflict his standard of morality on everyone else. What could be more Republican than that?

Chapter Ten

WWAD?

Acts of the Apostles

AUSTIN

Hello, it's me. I'm back. Did you miss me?

It's not often one gets a chance to participate in a world-changing event. Jesus did it. Neil Armstrong did it. And now I've done it. I always wondered what I would say if I was ever given the opportunity to do something amazing and possibly miraculous. And you gotta admit, returning from the dead is, at the very least, pretty cool. I can't think of anyone else who's done it, except for Jesus. And maybe Dick Clark. Definitely Shirley MacLaine.

So I say again—did you miss me? Okay, it's not "one small step for man, one giant leap for mankind." Sue me. I'm new at this. I've never died and come back to life before.

Wow. Just typing those words—with a complete set of brand-new born-again fingers!—gives me the shingles. But that's what happened. I died and came back to life. I was literally born again.

And I got the whole deal too. I saw the white light you always hear about, and I headed straight for it. At first you think, "Oh God, it's a train!" But it's not. The light is white because it's pure and encompasses everything there is. In the color spectrum, white is the combination of all colors. In the heavenly spectrum, white is the presence of God.

Let me apologize immediately for using such loaded religious words as "heavenly" and "God." I don't mean them in any specifically Judeo-Christian way. They are simply the only words I have to describe what happened to me.

I ascended into (sorry) heaven. I'm gonna call it heaven because that's what it seemed like to me. You can call it anything you like: limbo, nirvana, even Pittsburgh (although I've been to Pittsburgh and trust me—it ain't heaven). Heaven's a place, but it's not a place you can see, like it's full of clouds with angels sitting on them. Nor is it like this ethereal bus terminal. Nor (thank God) is it like Pittsburgh. It is at once no place and every place. It is nowhere and at the same time it's everywhere. It is nothing and at the same time it's everything.

I know, I know. Could I be more vague? It's probably more accurate to say that heaven is less a place than it is a state of mind. Dying and going to heaven is like achieving perfect understanding. The first words you say to yourself upon reaching heaven are "Oh, *now* I get it."[14] Everything suddenly makes sense.

Oh, and God. Like heaven, God isn't a person. He isn't an old guy with a white beard. Nor is he a woman. He's not even a he. God is ageless and sexless, omniscient and omnipresent. Like heaven, God is perfect and total clarity, complete understanding.

And dying and going to heaven and *coming back to life?* With all this perfect clarity and understanding? That's winning the lottery, man. That's having your cake and eating it too. That's Tippecanoe *and* Tyler. Too!

I admit, though, when I first came back, I freaked people out, starting with the gravedigger (or, in the more precise terminology of his profession, "burial attendant") who fainted dead away when I clawed my way out of my grave and said, "Hey, six more weeks of winter."

My wife was another one. She had already moved on to

[14] I know those are the first words because while I was up there I asked around. Everybody says it.

her trophy husband and was *not* happy to see me again. He's a nice guy though: good looking, plays the wacky neighbor on a sitcom that looks like it might get picked up. They got a house in the Valley so they're doing fine.

My son brought me in for show-and-tell where, if I do say so myself, I made a *very* big impression. I'm pretty sure I'm the only dad there who's died and come back to life. One dad came close, though—he'd been to Pittsburgh and back.

My son's teacher came up to me reverently and asked if she could touch my raiment. I apologized, telling her that I don't wear raiments and wouldn't know where to buy them if I did.

But her simple question sparked a realization in me. I now had a responsibility to spread the word. On the one hand, this bugged me. There's nothing I used to hate more than people trying to persuade you to believe the way they do. On the other hand, it seemed a little ungrateful to return from the dead and keep it to myself. I've never seen Miss Manners write a column on the etiquette of past-life/present-reincarnation proselytizing. Nor, apparently, does Hallmark make a specific card for someone who's come back to life. Some cute birthday cards, though.

So I called the local TV stations to try to get the word out. I don't know if you're familiar with video journalism in southern California, but the local television news here in Los Angeles is the worst in the country. Think "America's Funniest Fatal Accident Videos," but with less class. If they don't have any videotape to illustrate the story, it ain't news. They sent a camera crew out and I got no further than "Well, I died and came back . . ." before they cut away to their fourth freeway chase in twenty minutes.

I suspect, however, you already know the real obstacle I was facing. I was having the same problem every prophet who's come before me has had.

Everyone thinks I'm completely out of my mind.

I don't blame them. If I were them and they were me, telling me they had died and come back to life, I'd tell them to go back to East Nowhere, Nebraska, where people believe this hogwash because there's nothing to do there but hallucinate over the fumes of bad moonshine.

Nice guy, huh? That was the old me, a pseudo-sophisticated left coast bigot biased against the great unwashed of the vast flyover known as Middle America, particularly the good people of the great Cornhusker State.[15] Now I was one of these crackers. Just another nut job with a ridiculous story to peddle.

It's a national concern, really. Any screwball, ex-con, psychic, or pathetic inbreed can get a voice on TV. But if you actually have a by-God authentic religious resurrection, you can't get arrested. Unless, of course, you've got some compelling videotape, preferably shot during spring break in front of a wet T-shirt contest featuring drunken coeds shaking pixilated breasts. Then your resurrection will be on every single network during sweeps week. In prime time. They'll air that puppy till the cows come home. And the cows will have pixilated udders.

Clearly, since I lacked those audiovisual aids, I needed a disciple.

I reread the Acts of the Apostles and saw how the word of Jesus spread around the known world and became the religion of Christianity. Christianity didn't spread through the three P's: prayer, preaching, or proselytizing. Christianity was spread through the one V: vaudeville.

Critics of TV, music, and the movies always complain that the electronic media have a compelling and pervasive influence on the minds of America. They're right, of course. Producers deny it, but at the same time sell their commercial time for millions of dollars based on the very premise they disavow. Face it: a good story or a nice tune makes disparate, even dangerous, ideas easier to accept. Mary Poppins knew it when she sang, "A spoonful of sugar helps the medicine go down." The Communists knew it when they used Hollywood

---

[15]And Ohio. Don't get me started on Ohio.

movies to disseminate their subversive propaganda.[16] And the apostles knew it too. They knew the best way to spread the Lord's word was through the words of the mighty Abraham himself:

> A little song, a little dance
> A little seltzer down your pants

So the apostles took their acts on the road.

The story of Saul's conversion to Christianity is told by an old-fashioned double-act, that famous comedy team of Saul and Jesus, who sing:

> We're off on the road to Damascus
> We feared each other, but now we're fine
> If you want our advice then just ask us
> We'll turn your water into wine

In the course of their journey, Saul and Jesus do all the old jokes, which of course back then were new and cutting-edge. Jesus says to Saul, "I felt the Holy Spirit. D'you?" And Saul responds, "I heard that! You called me a Jew, didn't you? D'you? Jew?" Later, when Saul converts, he looks back on his own anti-Christian behavior and says, "I'm appalled." Jesus tells him, "Then that shall be your new name. Paul." Believe me, two thousand years ago, people ate this stuff up with a spoon.

But it wasn't only this sophisticated wordplay that so tickled the Middle East. There was also the lowbrow slapstick of the Holy Spirit itself. Every time the Holy Spirit arrives, it is accompanied by the sound of a "mighty wind" (Acts 2:2). Come on! Fart jokes are *always* funny. This was two millennia before Mel Brooks's infamous eating beans around the campfire scene in *Blazing Saddles*. You can only imagine how outrageous it must have been back then. And when the disci-

---

[16]Just because Senator Joe McCarthy (R-Wis.) was an evil, perverted demagogue doesn't mean he was wrong.

ples started speaking in tongues, it was a great excuse to utter nonsense gibberish that enabled them to stick out their tongues and make silly faces. Audiences were rolling in the aisles. At one show, they converted three thousand people at a single performance. And this was a matinee!

But mainly it was the magic that won over the nonbelievers. Jesus' disciples started walking around with flames burning over their heads, supposedly symbolizing the presence of the Holy Spirit. This was accompanied by fire eating and fire juggling and led to the mistaken belief that while filming his Pepsi commercial, Michael Jackson was briefly filled with the Holy Spirit.

Then Philip performed some "miracles" in Samaria. He healed the sick, changed some loaves into fishes, water into wine. Standard stuff, but impressive. Jesus named Peter "the Rock" and he became an incredibly famous wrestler. But because he could only do one thing—raise his eyebrow—his popularity diminished and he was forced to start the country's most successful dog act. Things took a tragic turn, however, when at one performance Stephen was trapped in a box when the saw-a-man-in-half trick went horribly wrong, and he became the first Christian martyr.

I knew if I was ever going to get the word out about what had happened to me, and what awaits us in the hereafter, I couldn't do it myself. For one thing, people wouldn't listen. For another, it's just pushy.

So I settled on Roger. The apostle Roger.

Roger's a stand-up. He tells a few jokes and does a few magic tricks, but mostly he's terrible. What he's always needed is a hook. He's an old friend, so under the guise of helping him out with his material, I told him what had happened to me, about how I got leprosy and died and came back to life. His reaction was typical.

He thought it was the funniest thing he had ever heard.

But it gave him his hook. He started incorporating "this guy I know, Austin" into his act, this atheist who becomes divine. At first nobody laughed and a few people actually booed (as the nonbelievers will). But then Roger got to the meat of his act. Roger told the crowd that whenever he's confused and he doesn't know what to do, he always asks himself one simple question:

What would Austin do?

This was his hook, his catchphrase. *What would Austin do?* He said it like ten times every gig. *What would Austin do?* He said it on Leno, brought down the house. He said it on Letterman and Dave wiped tears of hysteria off his face. Roger interspersed "What would Austin do?" in amongst the magic tricks and the fart jokes as a kind of religious seasoning. It was on bumper stickers and T-shirts. It became the catchphrase of a generation, the "Where's the beef?" of the new millennium.

It didn't hurt that Roger was Jewish. I mean, all comedians are Jewish, obviously; it's just one of the many ways that Jews run the world. But his conversion to Austinity therefore had a much stronger resonance. People subconsciously understood that Roger was somehow connected to Saul and his own conversion to Paul. (Roger didn't change his name, though. He was only now getting famous as Roger. Too much marketing confusion changing names in the middle of a rush to the top of the show biz ladder. Ask Roseanne Barr Arnold Burton Fortensky. Plus, it's just a great disciple-sounding name—Roger. Hey, and did you know that in England *roger* is a verb? True story.)

Anyway, people were buying it. Sure, they thought it was a gag, but it was a gag they liked and wanted to believe. Sort of like when you see Ted Koppel interviewing Kermit the Frog. Yeah, Kermit's a puppet but Ted *believes he's real*. And by God, so do we.

And what exactly is the basic tenet of Austinity? What great truth did I learn from my brief sojourn to the Promised Land? Just this:

Everything's going to be fine.

That's it. It's so simple. We learn it as kids. It's one of the first things parents say to their children. But then the message gets diluted because we feel we have to qualify it. "Every-thing's going to be fine unless we get murdered in our beds by a crack-addict-welfare-mom-with-easy-access-to-a-handgun." But everything became clear to me up in heav—I mean, that incredibly clear place. There is a rhyme and rea-son to things. The answer to the question, "What would Austin do?" is usually this:

Nothing.

Why?

Because everything's going to be fine. It'll all work out in the end.

But because new converts are like children, I needed to make up some rules, sort of my own Several/Half-Dozen Commandments. In no particular order, they are:

Number 1: Thou shalt not give money to me or my followers.

That's pretty straightforward. I thought this should be made clear right at the top. People asking for money in my name are not true Austins.

Number 2: Thou shalt not commit violence in my name.

Again, you'd think this should be self-evident. I wish there were some way to enforce this, because *I'm* certainly not going to do it. The promise of hell, like the so-called deter-rent of the death penalty, sure doesn't do it. All I can do (through Roger) is lay down the law and hope for the best.

Number 3: Leave everybody else the hell alone.

This seems to me clearer and more to the point than "Do unto others as you would have them do unto you." Let's face it: there's a lot of tarnish on the so-called Golden Rule. Most people seem to only remember the first three words and do nothing *but* do unto others; they do unto others all day long. Others misinterpret it, thinking it means to do unto others *before* they do unto you. I think my Platinum Rule (I upgraded it) is more to the point. Keep to yourself. I *am* an island. Piss off.

Number 4: There shall be no ritual mutilation in my name.

This sort of falls under Number 3 and could really be called Number 3-B, but since I want to be clear, I'm giving it its own designation. I don't want there to be a kind of modern-day version of the Council of Jerusalem (Acts 15), where various Austin factions get together and argue about what it takes to be a real Austin. Let me spell it out: don't *under any circumstances* circumcise penises or clitorises, don't scar yourselves with tattoos (the fake ones that go on with water are acceptable), and don't pierce any part of your body. Hell, if it were up to me, I'd say don't even pierce your ears. It's moronic and unattractive and—wait a second, what am I saying? It *is* up to me!

Number 5: Don't pierce your ears.

Number 6: The only acceptable kosher foods are Cap'n Crunch cereal and Kraft Macaroni and Cheese.

I admit to a bias here, and nutrition experts may object, but this is comfort food of the highest order and I stand behind their inclusion here.

And that's it. I'm sure that at some point there'll be a movie made of my life (and death!). Roger and I will probably have a big fight over who gets to play me and we'll go our separate ways. Maybe I'll get to write the screenplay. I'll probably get some horrible back-end deal, where like the twelve tribes of Israel and the author of *Forrest Gump*, I'm promised something that doesn't exist, like Jerusalem or a percentage of the "profits."

But I don't know. I never claimed to be omniscient. I'm just Austin. What would I do?

Right now, I'm taking a break.

Chapter Eleven

The Epistles

The Little-Known
Responses to the Letters

REED

I'm angry. Really angry. This business of Austin being res-
urrected and becoming some kind of messiah has shaken
my faith to the core.

I'm angry because I know he's not making up this stuff. He
really has come back to life in a messianic kind of way. Oh
sure, I was dubious at first. I thought it was some kind of
trick, a big special effect that Austin was using to get attention or, more likely, to make light of my beliefs.

But now I know that it's no trick. I gave Austin succor as
he died slowly of leprosy (no, it still doesn't mean what
Austin thought it meant). I was really there for him, you
know what I mean? I saved each of his deformed extremities
as it withered and fell off, in the hope that perhaps they could
be reattached at a later date. I tried to comfort him and
encourage him to give his life to God before it was too late.
But then he died. It was too late. Or was it?

Reverend Alan always taught that there was only one way
to salvation and it was a long, hard road of self-denial and
sacrifice. And I believed it. Sure, over the years I had one or
two minor disagreements with the pastor, but I tried my
darndest to live my life the way he told me I should. And I'm
telling you it was tough. Then all of a sudden here comes
Austin, a new deity with a simple plan for salvation and

easier-to-follow commandments. What a sucker I've been. So I'm mad at Reverend Alan for leading me down the crooked, difficult path to God. I'm not so sure I'm going to try to be nice to him anymore.

I'm also mad at God. Why did he pick Austin to be His messenger? It doesn't make any sense. I'm not saying God is wrong, but Austin is a terrible choice for a messiah. He's an atheist, for God's sake! Or at least he was until recently. I, on the other hand, would have made an excellent messiah. I am extremely pious. I am extremely humble. I would gladly have rotted and died from leprosy to become the messenger. Well, maybe not gladly, but I would have done it. For goodness sake, I was the one who got Austin started on his spiritual quest when I agreed to write this book with him. And for this, God stabs me in the back and picks Austin. Maybe it's because I'm a Democrat.

And I'm mad at Austin. No, not because he came back as a savior. He was chosen. It was beyond his control. I'm angry because Austin picked Roger to be his disciple instead of me. I feel betrayed. After all we've been through together, he should have picked me. I just don't understand why he passed me over. He knows from firsthand experience that I'd be a great disciple. I spent years harassing him about God, trying to force him to believe the way I did. All of a sudden he gets one little spiritual insight—okay, a fairly significant spiritual insight—and does he bring it to me? No, he brings it to Roger. So I'm not going to be doing Austin any more favors. I don't care if he has an easy road to salvation.

I think Austin knows how I'm feeling because he wrote me a little note trying to convert me to Austinity and explain his choice of Roger as his disciple. Here's what I wrote back:

Dear Austin:

I got your letter. I appreciate that you are a busy guy these days, being the Messiah and all, but given our history it would have been nice if we could have talked about all this face-to-face. This would not have been difficult since you are now capable of being everywhere at once.

Thanks for the offer, but I have no interest in being your second disciple. The proposal seems like an afterthought to me. And I can't in good conscience promote you as the Messiah because, frankly, this resurrection thing has gone to your head. What sort of Messiah stabs his best friend in the back? Just because you're a deity doesn't make you better than everyone else.

I actually like much of the doctrine you espouse, but I refuse to become a tool to promote your aggrandizement. So I've decided to start my own sect of Austinity. I'm going to keep the parts that I like and dump the parts I don't. And to delineate my sect from Austinity, I'm calling it "Austianity."

I'm temporarily making you a prophet of Austianity for the sake of expedience. I've begun selling relics to cover start-up costs. I guess it would be more accurate to say that I'm selling your former body parts as relics—the ones that fell off from the leprosy. I saved them, remember? Once I've sold all the relics, I'll "discover" something sordid in your past and have you excommunicated.

Once you've been excommunicated, I'm going to have to discredit you in order to draw some attention. This will involve a media smear campaign. I apologize for this in advance, but since you are the Messiah I know you will forgive me.

Reverend Alan is my apostle and he's great. He's pretty much willing to do or say anything as long as I don't come within a two-mile radius of his home. It's just one of his idiosyncrasies, I guess. The medication seems to be keeping his mood swings under control. He still babbles unintelligibly from time to time, but I just tell everyone he's speaking in tongues. It's actually a great help with recruitment.

I'll sign off now. I'm going to Hollywood to try and convert some major stars. If I can get a few big names to sign on, the rest of LA will follow. You know actors. They'll do anything if they think it will help their careers.

Divinely yours,
Reed

I guess my note to Austin is an appropriate lead-in because this chapter is all about letters—in particular the Epistles, which were letters of instruction for the early Christians. Apart from the Gospels, the Acts of the Apostles, and the book of Revelation, they make up the entire New Testament. The Apostle Paul wrote most of these twenty-one letters. Before Paul became a red-hot born-again proselytizer, he hated Christians. Paul had a good deal in common with Austin. Other epistles were written by James, Peter, John, and Jude.

As I was writing back to Austin, I began to wonder whether the early Christians had written back to Paul in the same way and, if so, what they'd said. Perhaps you've never thought about this. I hadn't. But suddenly my curiosity was piqued.

Guess what? They did write back and these letters exist. You know who found them for me? My disciple, Reverend Alan, did. I accidentally bumped into him at Seven-Eleven. It wasn't a violation of the restraining order because the store is more than two miles from his house. The pastor is working the night shift and trying to ease his way back into normal society. He was rather surprised to see me and spent several minutes cowering in the corner. But when I asked him if he knew anything about responses to the Epistles he brightened up immediately. A twinkle came to his eye. He looked happier than I've seen him since I joined his congregation. Pastor said he knew where he could find such letters but that it would require him to leave the country. Reverend Alan said it might take a while, but he thought he could probably track down this missing correspondence somewhere in the Middle East. I told him I had a bit of extra cash from some relics I'd recently sold and would happily pay his expenses. He was absolutely elated and dashed off to his travel agent to buy the plane ticket. I think he was more excited than I was about the prospect of finding these letters.

I drove him to the airport the next morning. Just as I was starting to help him unload his bags, he dashed into the airport and out of sight. I love his enthusiasm. Several weeks later a packet arrived in the mail. In it were some papers and a note that said:

Dear Reed, I have found some of the missing responses to the Epistles. I translated them into English and they are enclosed. I am confident that I can track down the rest of them, but it will take some time. I will need to be out of the country for the foreseeable future. Please send more money. Faithfully yours, Reverend Alan.

P.S. Under no circumstances should you come to Israel to help me. I am doing just fine on my own. I take great comfort in the fact that we are on different continents separated by a major body of water.

The packet had apparently been misdirected by the postal service, because the postmark on it said "Tahiti." I wasn't sure what Reverend Alan meant about being comforted by our separation, but the letters that he enclosed were fascinating, so I wired him more money immediately.

I think these responses are self-explanatory, but just in case they aren't, let me preface them slightly. The writers of the Epistles were a little preachy and very opinionated. They pointed out every little mistake the new Christians were making both in daily life and at church. As you will see from the responses below, these criticisms were not always well received. In fact, Saint Paul rubbed so many important people the wrong way that he was imprisoned several times before finally being executed. On that bright note, here they are:

The *Romans* write back to Paul

Dear Paul, We received your long letter condemning homosexuality. As for all your advice, we were going to suggest you stick it where the sun doesn't shine, but that might constitute some of the behavior that you are so concerned about. You should be happy to learn that there are no longer any practicing homosexuals here in Rome. We've been practicing for so long that we finally have it perfected. Rehearsal is over. It's time to perform.

As you requested, we enclose money for your trip to Spain. We performed a drag show as a fundraiser. The all-male Carmen Miranda chorus brought the house down with their rendition of the song "YMCA."

The Romans

The *Corinthians* write back to Paul

Paul, Please don't write us again. The women of our congregation found your letters. They are furious that you have ordered them to keep quiet in church and obey the men. They have gone on strike. Our lives are miserable. You will be delighted to know that we are now "in charge" of everything—diaper changes, cooking, cleaning, etc. They're holding out on us too, if you get our drift. The only person who's getting any is that poor old redneck that you told us we had to excommunicate for sleeping with his stepmother.

We found it odd that you claim in the letter that you don't preach for profit and then asked us for money. Nonetheless, we performed a drag show as a fundraiser for you. The all-male Carmen Miranda chorus brought the house down with their rendition of the song "YMCA."

The Men of Corinth

The *Galatians* write back to Paul

Paul, As per your advice, we are no longer paying attention to the missionary who told us that we needed to follow all the old Jewish laws including circumcision. You seemed quite angry that he tried to lead us astray when you said you hoped that the missionary would "cut off much more" than just his foreskin. Anyway, we followed your suggestion and cut off the penis of the missionary. Word of this Christian rite has spread like wildfire through the region. Strangely enough, since then we have had a great deal of trouble finding new converts. On a bright note, our all-male choir is now able to reach the high notes much more easily.

The Galatians

The *Philippians* write back to Paul

Paul, You are very welcome for the gifts you received in prison. At the moment we are putting together a second package with all of the items you requested. It should not be difficult to bake a file into a cake. What flavor frosting would you like? We have been unable to locate the September issue of Playboy *featuring "The*

Subservient Women of the Early Church" layout, but we will keep looking.
  The Philippians

The *Colossians* write back to Paul

Paul, Thanks for the note. Glad to hear that you are making so many friends in prison. Can you clarify for us how you can be somebody's "girlfriend"? Thanks for the etching. It looks like you have been spending a lot of time at the gym. Who would have thought you'd have so much "free" time in prison? Get it? Free *time? Ha, ha. Sorry for the bad pun.*
  The Colossians

The *Thessalonians* write back to Paul

Paul, Before your note we'd all been in committed monogamous married relationships, but your very graphic warnings about sexual deviancy have given us a lot of new ideas about combinations and positions. I guess you're kind of a missionary of the nonmissionary, if you get our drift. Regarding the third perversion you discussed: How do we keep the sheep from running away?

Thanks also for the heads-up that Christ is returning soon. We've all quit our jobs and are just partying until the big day.
  The Thessalonians

Timothy writes back to Paul

Paul, I was shocked and dismayed when I read your letter. I thought you'd lost your mind. Then I realized that you were pulling my leg! You are such a card! I cracked up at all the stuff about women being silent in church and not telling men what to do. Here's a wacky idea for a prank letter to the Ephesians. Tell them that only men can become priests and that they will have to remain celibate!! That'll freak them out. Ha, ha.

Thanks for all the pastoring tips. Yes, I will always try to keep the sermons short on Super Bowl Sunday.

I am happy to report that things for me here seem to be much better than things for you in prison. I don't think I can visit you in

Rome because it is awfully difficult to find someone to fill in for me on Sundays. As you know, there are only a handful of pastors in the entire world.

I'm also sorry to hear that you don't have any friends. This is probably because you've spent the latter part of your life condemning everyone you came in contact with. I'm no prophet, but I could see this coming. Anyway, hang in there (maybe an unfortunate choice of words). If I don't get to Rome, I'll see you on the other side.

Timothy

The *Hebrews* write back to Paul

Paul, Thanks for encouraging us in our new faith. We agree that Jesus is better than angels, prophets, Moses, high priests, and animal sacrifices, although we might not have put it in those exact terms. Thanks also for pointing out that, "Jesus is better than a kick in the teeth or a sharp blow to the head."

Cautiously yours, The Hebrews

A Christian writes back to *James*

James, Thanks for the note. It's always good to hear from Jesus' younger brother. Or rather, as you continually point out, Jesus' younger half-brother. An overachieving sibling is always a tough act to follow. Everyone expects you to be perfect.

By the way, did his Father come to visit every other weekend? I hope you are making progress in your therapy.

Best wishes, A concerned Christian

The Turks write back to *Peter*

Peter, Thanks for the tip on spotting false teachers. We did not realize that they engage in orgies. We are going to as many orgies as we can to locate all the false teachers. It's a tough job, but it's got to be done.

Turkish Christians

A Christian writes back to *John*

John, I have taken your advice and excommunicated everyone that was adding on to the basic Christian doctrine. I have expelled all the Mormons, Scientologists, Christian Scientists, Jehovah's Witnesses, everyone who reads horoscopes or uses feng shui, and those who phone the psychic hotline. I am now the only remaining member of the church. It's good to know that Jesus was fully human as well as fully spiritual. I'm hoping he will stop by and visit me. I'm lonely.

An isolated Christian

A Christian writes back to *Jude*

Hey Jude, I wanted to drop a note to your brother, Jesus, but I don't have his address so I'm writing to you instead. Please pass along to him the message that we are all extremely grateful that he forgives our sins. We look at his forgiveness as a kind of cosmic "Get Out of Jail Free" card. We just sin like crazy and then ask forgiveness. It's great! Your brother is the coolest. Stop by any time. We'd love to party with you.

A grateful Christian

P.S. Bring booze and broads

Before I conclude this chapter I'd like to thank Reverend Alan for uncovering these priceless letters. They will be invaluable in bringing both legitimacy and converts (not to mention their hard-earned cash) to my new religion—Austianity. These letters are true treasures that had been lost for two thousand years. And so is my pastor. A true treasure, I mean. He hasn't been lost for two thousand years. That's what this book is really all about—lost treasures.

I'm planning a big surprise for Reverend Alan to thank him for this amazing discovery. I'm going to track him down wherever he is (even if it's Tahiti!) and personally help him find the rest of these letters. If he knew I was planning to do this I know he'd protest. He's so diligent that he doesn't want me to waste my valuable time on a wild goose chase. But maybe spending a couple of years travelling the world together will bring us closer than we already are. Sure, we might drive each other a little crazy, but I want to help. It's the Christian thing to do.

Chapter Twelve

Revelation

It's the End
of the World as We Know It

AUSTIN

Here's what impresses me most about God. He starts out as such a tough guy in the Old Testament but in the New Testament becomes loving and forgiving. In my mind, this is an improvement. God betters Himself as He goes along.

I only wish I could say the same thing about myself.

The rise of Austinity has been hit with a backlash. It was inevitable, I suppose. I was the flavor of the month and everybody was talking about me, asking themselves and each other "What would Austin do?" until somebody—I'm pretty sure Keith Richards was the first—said in an interview, "Who *cares* what Austin would do?"[17]

That started the ball rolling. My ex-wife came out with a book called "What Austin *Can't* Do," which went on for close to eight hundred pages and became a best-seller. Roger turned on me too, denouncing me on *Oprah*. This was doubly aggravating, because I had been pestering Oprah's people for months to feature me as an author on her book club. Despite my glowing dedication in the opening of this book,

---

[17]Keith was still pissed that Elton John made so much money off his rewrite of "Candle in the Wind" for Princess Diana—"songs for dead blondes," in Keith's phrase. Still, as if he somehow might be misinterpreted, Keith added for emphasis, "I think that guy Austin's a bloody wanker."

they refused to book me. Maybe it was because I described the story of my resurrection as "one woman's struggle against incredible odds to find her true spirit." Oprah herself sent a message to me that not only was my book unacceptable, but that my message of "leave each other alone, everything will be fine" was, in her own words, "more dangerous than hamburger." I thought about suing her but that seemed to go against my own Platinum Rule. And besides, she may have a point.

I don't really blame Roger, though. In his defense, Roger saw the tide turning and decided to jump off the train and fly to safety. He feared that people would confuse the message with the messenger in the same way that he confused his tide/train/flying metaphors. He was under increasing pressure to deny me, so I don't blame him in the least. He did what he had to do.

The biggest surprise, though, was Reed.

He was very shaken up when I died. I mean genuinely upset, and not just because it looked as if he'd have to finish this book by himself. When I suddenly reappeared he wasn't pleased or surprised, only suspicious, as if I'd gone to a spa for three weeks and managed to use cocktail wieners to fake my stubby, leprosy-laden fingers. I thought he'd be the first one to believe me because of his childlike, rock-solid faith. Instead, my reappearance seemed to throw him for a theological loop. The good news was that his confusion allowed him to make another visit to his pastor, which I know he enjoys.

The bad news was that he was the first "Austin expert" the media came to for information. Roger may have been my Peter (now *there's* a phrase you don't read every day), but Reed was something worse.

Reed was the Antiaustin.

It wasn't that he thought I was a phony. He was just horrified by my transformation into the founder of a religious movement. Me, a former atheist. He thought it was unfair. He was right, of course, but it wasn't my fault. I didn't *ask* to be born again. Reed started saying, as frequently and loudly and to as many people as he could, that not only is everything *not* going to be fine, but that people need to take action *now*, leave no stone unturned, no action untaken, no pastor unconsulted. He turned it into a fight. He made a simple difference in theological philosophy a personal battle for ultimate power. The same way Satan did. And, in a slightly different context, George Steinbrenner.

I didn't take it well. I got extremely angry. I didn't know what to do. I didn't really have a place to put my anger.

But then I read about God's behavior in Revelation, and all became clear.

Revelation was written by John, in which he describes his "visions" of the future. His visions are bizarre and horrifying and—to many people—clearly drug-induced. These are the same people who accuse the Beatles of filling "I Am the Walrus" with secret drug references.[18] It's true that early practitioners often described a mind-expanding clarity after using LSD (or so I'm told) that resembled a religious trance. But a true apocalyptic vision is slightly different than staring at your fingernail and going, "Whoa."

So I am here to testify that John wrote the truth. Since I walked the walk I can verify that John talks the talk. The endtime will be much as he described it. At least if I have anything to say about it.

John's first vision describes his divine insight into seven prominent churches in Turkey (Revelation 4:1–5:14). I know, you're thinking, what does this have to do with the price of chilis in Fremont? It's not the churches that are important, it's the number. Seven is a very powerful number. Seven symbolizes completion. It's no accident that God created the world in seven days. You've heard the expression "lucky seven." Seven pays off the best when shooting craps. I always get lucky on my seventh date. The finest movie ever made is *Seven Brides for Seven Brothers*. The examples are endless.

---

[18]This is ridiculous. The Beatles only did that with "Yesterday."

Then John sees God holding a scroll locked with seven seals. Suddenly, seven trumpets blast and the seven seals balance seven balls on their seven noses. John sees a vision of the Seven Horsemen of the Apocalypse: War, Famine, Disease, Conquest, Boils, Hemorrhoids, and Sneezy. And we're off to the races.

John then describes the ultimate battle between good and evil. He pictures a royal rider on a white horse, leading the army of heaven into battle against the forces of evil. Many people interpret this rider to be the King of Kings, Jesus Christ himself. I think it's clear now that John was describing me. John predicted my rise. My coming was foretold. I am the Eggman. Goo-goo-g'joob.

John's description of my great evil nemesis should now also be obvious in light of recent events. Some scholars interpret the hideous monster born of Satan to be a thinly veiled reference to the Roman Empire. Others believe it describes the Antichrist. I think it's clear that John is really describing Reed Martin. The Antiaustin.

Again, let's go to the numbers. Reed's full name, Reed Campbell Martin, has eighteen letters in it. When you divide eighteen by three (the most powerful number, being the number of the Holy Trinity as well as the ideal number of Stooges and Marx Brothers), you get six. Reed's name therefore consists of three sixes—666, the mark of the Antiaustin.[19]

Austin ultimately vanquishes the Antiaustin in Revelation and the stage is set for Judgment Day, wherein the Book of Life (in this case, *TV Guide*) is opened and those not contained therein are found wanting and cast into a lake of fire. Scholars debate whether this means a literal lake of flaming sulfur, or merely separation from Austin. I'll tell you what it means. It means that anyone displeasing to me (meaning Reed, Roger, and Oprah, among others) will be cast into Lake Erie or anyplace along the Cuyahoga River.[20] They can

---

[19]The fact that my full name, Austin Kent Tichenor, also has eighteen letters in it is just a coincidence.

[20]I told you. Don't get me started on Ohio.

either burn or drown; it matters not to me. I can't do anything about it. So it is written, so it shall be done.

Then will come a new heaven and earth. But I won't call it heaven. Having vanquished my foes and the nonbelievers, I'll want to start afresh and do away with the old terminology. Instead of calling it heaven, we'll call it "Club Heaven," where the drinks are free, the bikinis are thonged, and the only men wearing Speedos are the ones with washboard abs who can really do them justice.

And I and my people will settle in for eternity. Anyone and everyone from any former religion will be welcome, so long as they forswear age-old prejudice and tribal warfare.

And the Word shall go forth across the land:

Relax.

Leave each other alone.

Everything's going to be fine.

But nobody better mention the name *Reed Martin*. That would make me very wroth. Make me smite somebody's ass.

Backword

A Note of Explanation
REED

Austin Tichenor has been locked up in a secure mental care facility outside Phoenix. With regular medication and proper psychoanalysis, his delusions of divinity have significantly diminished. He is no longer considered a threat to anyone but himself.

Austin shares a cell with Reverend Alan Knudsen, who was flown to Phoenix via Red Cross jet from Tahiti where I found him in a state of total disorientation.

I write this from my villa overlooking the French Riviera. Austianity has made me an extremely wealthy man. I have definitely discovered untold treasures in the Bible. Ka-ching!

Bibliography

Even a semiautobiographical work such as this is reliant on years of research. Unfortunately, we had neither the time nor the inclination for that, so we only gave a cursory glance to the following:

Holy Bible. King James Version.

How to Get into the Bible by Stephen M. Miller. Thomas Nelson Publishers.

The Illustrated Guide to the Bible by J. R. Porter. Oxford University Press.

NIV Compact Bible Commentary by John Sailhamer. Zondervan Publishing House.

NIV Compact Dictionary of the Bible by J. D. Douglas and Merrill C. Tenney. Zondervan Publishing House.

Additional Resources

Are You There, God? It's Me, Margaret by Judy Blume. Scholastic Books.

Curious George Evolves into the Man in the Big Yellow Hat by Charles Darwin, with apologies to H. A. Rey. Galapagos Press.

Dave Berg Looks at the Lighter Side of Eternal Damnation by Dave Berg. Mad Magazine Publications.

Devil in Miss Jones. X-rated version. Creamy Home Videos. VHS.

Jesus Christ Superstar by Andrew Lloyd Webber and Tim Rice. Original cast album. MCA Records.

Oh God! by Larry Gelbart. VHS, laserdisc.

Paradise Lost by John Milton. A Children's Pop-Up Book. Weekly Reader Press.

Private Mental-Health Facilities in the American Southwest by R. U. Knuttz. Loonybin Press.

Index